T0114859

GRADES **4–8**

Fluency
The READING PUZZLE

Elaine K. McEwan
Kathie Ward Dobberteen
Q. L. Pearce

CORWIN PRESS
Classroom

For information:

Corwin Press
A SAGE Company
2455 Teller Road
Thousand Oaks, California 91320
CorwinPress.com

SAGE, Ltd.
1 Oliver's Yard
55 City Road
London EC1Y 1SP
United Kingdom

SAGE India Pvt. Ltd.
B 1/I 1 Mohan Cooperative
Industrial Area
Mathura Road, New Delhi
India 110 044

SAGE Asia-Pacific Pvt. Ltd.
33 Pekin Street #02-01
Far East Square
Singapore 048763

ISBN: 978-1-4129-5828-8

This book is printed on acid-free paper.

08 09 10 11 12 10 9 8 7 6 5 4 3 2 1

Executive Editor: Kathleen Hex
Managing Developmental Editor: Christine Hood
Editorial Assistant: Anne O'Dell
Developmental Writers: Kathie Ward Dobberteen and Q. L. Pearce
Developmental Editor: June Hetzel
Proofreader: Carrie Reiling
Art Director: Anthony D. Paular
Design Project Manager: Jeffrey Stith
Cover Designers: Michael Dubowe and Jeffrey Stith
Illustrator: Reggie Holladay
Design Consultant: The Development Source

GRADES **4–8**

TABLE OF CONTENTS

Connections to Standards

This chart shows the national language arts standards covered in this book.

LANGUAGE ARTS	Standards are covered on pages
Read a wide range of print and nonprint texts to build an understanding of texts, of self, and of the cultures of the United States and the world; to acquire new information; to respond to the needs and demands of society and the workplace; and for personal fulfillment (includes fiction and nonfiction, classic, and contemporary works).	14, 15, 29, 36, 42, 63
Read a wide range of literature from many periods in many genres to build an understanding of the many dimensions (e.g., philosophical, ethical, aesthetic) of human experience.	14, 15, 29, 36, 42, 63
Apply a wide range of strategies to comprehend, interpret, evaluate, and appreciate texts. Draw on prior experience, interactions with other readers and writers, knowledge of word meaning and of other texts, word identification strategies, and understanding of textual features (e.g., sound-letter correspondence, sentence structure, context, graphics).	9, 14, 16, 22, 23, 29, 36, 42, 63, 67
Adjust the use of spoken, written, and visual language (e.g., conventions, style, vocabulary) to communicate effectively with a variety of audiences and for different purposes.	15, 16, 23, 29, 36, 42, 63, 67, 74
Use spoken, written, and visual language to accomplish a purpose (e.g., for learning, enjoyment, persuasion, and the exchange of information).	15, 16, 23, 29, 36, 42, 63, 74

978-1-4129-5828-8

Introduction

Dear Teachers,

When Dr. McEwan asked me to write about my experiences as part of this book, I was happy to relate how her reading strategies improved the reading skills of students at my school. Only 42% of our students were reading at and above grade level when I began my tenure as principal of La Mesa Dale Elementary School in La Mesa, California. Our students would never be able to break out of the cycle of poverty if things remained the same at our Title I school. Reading, although an important aspect of the educational process, was not a focus. It was treated with a remedial flavor—putting Band-Aids® on small groups of students who were experiencing difficulties. We had great teachers who taught well and cared deeply for their students but no common, systematic focus.

We knew that change was needed and initially grasped at anything that was new. First, we taught multicultural education, hoping to build acceptance and tolerance among our culturally diverse population. Then, we emphasized conflict resolution to encourage respect, self reliance, and student ownership of what took place at school. None of these programs had any impact on student achievement whatsoever. Fortunately, at about this time, we attended a workshop on reading given by Dr. Elaine McEwan. She described the Reading Puzzle, which is a way of organizing and understanding reading instruction. The puzzle contains the essential reading skills that students need to master in order to become literate at every grade level. After looking at the puzzle, it was clear that we were missing some essential pieces. We had finally found our unifying vision.

The first component we put in place was an explicit phonological awareness program for kindergarten and first-grade students. At the end of the year, after teaching phonological awareness in kindergarten and first grade, the percentage of first-grade students reading at and above grade level improved from 55% to 88%. After that amazing success, we felt we were really onto something. We focused on other areas of the Reading Puzzle, and incredibly enough, we were on the right path. For example, we made sure our students were reading a lot and had a reading incentive program in which our goal was to read enough books that, when stacked together, would reach the height of the Sea World tower. Our students reached their goal, and we took the entire school to Sea World to celebrate. After decoding mastery, we started focusing on cognitive strategies so students could obtain a greater depth of understanding of what they were reading. We built a reading culture in which reading took place every single day of the school year.

978-1-4129-5828-8

After several years of incremental growth, we were close to having 90% of students reading at and above grade level, as measured by individual running records. Although we were almost delirious with excitement, we still had a big dilemma on our hands. We were scoring very well on our state-mandated tests but not as well as we should have with such a high percentage of truly excellent readers. We started doing some additional research and looked more closely at those students who were reading well above grade level on our individual reading tests but were scoring at or below grade level on the standardized tests. We found that we needed to work more explicitly on one of the pieces of the Reading Puzzle that we had put on the back burner.

We discovered that every one of our students who scored high on individual tests, and yet scored below grade level on standardized tests, also scored below grade level expectations on reading fluency. Finally, we found both our problem and our solution. We began working on fluency with these students, and they, in turn, began scoring well on the standardized tests. We ended up with 92% of students reading at and above grade level. We also scored extremely high on our state-mandated tests. We did so well that we became one of 96 National Title I Distinguished Schools in the country and were one of six schools in the nation to receive the Chase School Change Award from the Secretary of the Department of Education at Lincoln Center in New York City.

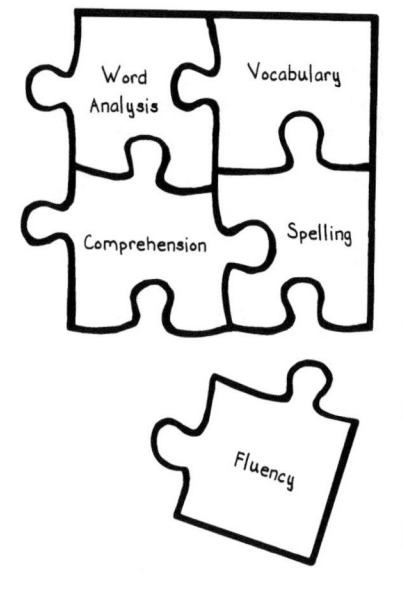

You, too, can use the Reading Puzzle to focus your vision and ensure that you "teach them all to read." *The Reading Puzzle, Grades 4–8* series is derived from Dr. McEwan's bestselling *Teach Them All to Read: Catching the Kids Who Fall Through the Cracks* (2002). It focuses on five of the essential components of successful reading instruction: Word Analysis, Vocabulary, Spelling, Comprehension, and Fluency. Use this series as a guide to systematically put in place each of these components. This book is designed to support reading fluency instruction, a critical, but sometimes neglected piece of the puzzle in successful reading instruction, particularly in grades 4–8.

Good luck with your reading journey!

Sincerely,

Kathie Ward Dobberteen, Retired Principal
La Mesa Dale Elementary School, La Mesa, California

How to Use This Book

This resource book is designed to provide the strategies and activities that will help develop your students' reading fluency. In order for students to reach grade-level expectancies in the number of words read correctly per minute by the end of the year, they need frequent practice. Fortunately, fluency lessons do not take much time and are easy to prepare and teach. Fluency is simple to measure, and progress is readily apparent.

In my book, *Teach Them All to Read: Catching the Kids Who Fall Through the Cracks* (2002), I describe fluency as a frequently neglected piece of the Reading Puzzle. I explain several important methods for developing fluency and recommend that students learn many sight words well and also read many different kinds of texts in lots of different ways both at home and at school. I also discuss a number of strategies that can improve fluency. These strategies can be categorized in several groups according to Timothy Rasinski (2003), including: 1) modeling good oral reading, 2) providing oral support for readers, 3) offering plenty of practice opportunities, and 4) encouraging fluency through phrasing.

Kathie Ward Dobberteen has taken my book, *Teach Them All to Read* (2002), and developed this derivative work, *Fluency, Grades 4–8*, to make research-based fluency activities accessible to all teachers. Each activity and lesson supports students' fluency development. In addition, samples of engaging, high-interest passages, authored by Q. L. Pearce, accompany the lessons. Many passages can be applied with several strategies and utilized across grade levels. Passages were leveled utilizing the Flesch-Kincaid readability formula with minor adaptations. Passage levels were adjusted when the passages contained key repeated multisyllabic terms and proper nouns (e.g., *Antarctica*). These one or two key word(s) per passage, essential to meaning and recognized through configuration, sometimes dramatically skewed the grade-level rating.

Passage levels are coded at the bottom of each page using the symbols shown below. Enjoy *Fluency, Grades 4–8*. Happy teaching!

|4| = Grade 4 |5| = Grade 5 |6| = Grade 6

|7| = Grade 7 |8| = Grade 8

978-1-4129-5828-8

Put It Into Practice

What is fluency? The National Reading Panel determined that fluent readers can read text with speed, accuracy, and proper expression (Rasinski, 2003). Fluency is highly correlated with the ability to comprehend what is read (Fuchs, Fuchs, Hops, & Jenkins, 2001). In fact, measures of oral reading have been found to be more highly correlated with reading comprehension scores than were measures of silent reading rates in a sample of children whose reading skills varied across a broad range (Jenkins, Fuchs, Espin, Van den Broek, & Deno, 2000). As students develop fluency in their oral reading, comprehension scores improve.

According to Allington (1983), fluent oral readers, even with similar knowledge of the vocabulary and concepts in the text as their peers, are better able to understand what they read than are their dysfluent peers. Focusing too much attention on word recognition drains cognitive resources, impeding comprehension. Fluency enhances comprehension.

Fluent Reader

Finally, the little island poked above the waves.

Dysfluent Reader

F-F-F-Fin-Finley, the-the li-little ...is ...is ...land ...is land? What does that mean?

The National Research Council concluded, "Adequate progress in learning to read English (or any other alphabetic language) beyond the initial level depends on *sufficient practice to achieve fluency* [italics added] with different texts" (Snow, Burns, & Griffin, 1998, p. 223). The report also recommends that "because the ability to obtain meaning from print depends so strongly on the development of accurate word recognition and reading fluency, both should be regularly assessed in the classroom, permitting *timely and effective instructional response* [italics added] when difficulty or delay is apparent" (p. 7).

978-1-4129-5828-8

CHAPTER 1

Learn Lots of Sight Words Well

Students can improve reading fluency by learning lots of sight words well. Sight words, although originally phonetically decoded by the reader, have been read so frequently that they are now read fluently without attention to the letters in the words. Learning sight words usually takes practice to reach a level of automaticity. Practice in reading single words leads to increased fluency when those words are later found in text, and many words can be learned through simple flashcard repetition. Many enjoyable games can be played with flashcards, as long as they are efficient and provide lots of word repetitions per session.

Fast Blast! (Grades 4–6)

"Fast Blast!" is a reading activity that ensures students can decode sight words with a high level of automaticity. The goal is to correctly decode 25 words in 15–20 seconds.

1. Working in groups of three, have students read the **Sight Word List reproducibles (pages 11–13)**. During each session, one student is the timer, one student is the assessor, and one student checks words for correct pronunciation.

2. The assessor highlights a word if the student being tested cannot quickly decode the word or misreads the word.

3. Each student participates in each role until all three students have read the current list. Students record each successfully completed list.

Read It! Read It! (Grades 4–5)

"Read It! Read It!" is a homework program that ensures students learn high-frequency words with the necessary level of automaticity.

1. Send home the **Read It! Read It! Parent Letter reproducible (page 10)**.

2. Start students with the list at their level and sequentially proceed through the lists.

3. Invite tutors to test students on sight words from the previous week's list. When students pass with 100%, acknowledge their achievement and give them a new list. If students miss some words, highlight those words and send home the list again with a short note.

4. Chart students' progress and present students with awards or certificates when they pass all the lists.

Read It! Read It! Parent Letter

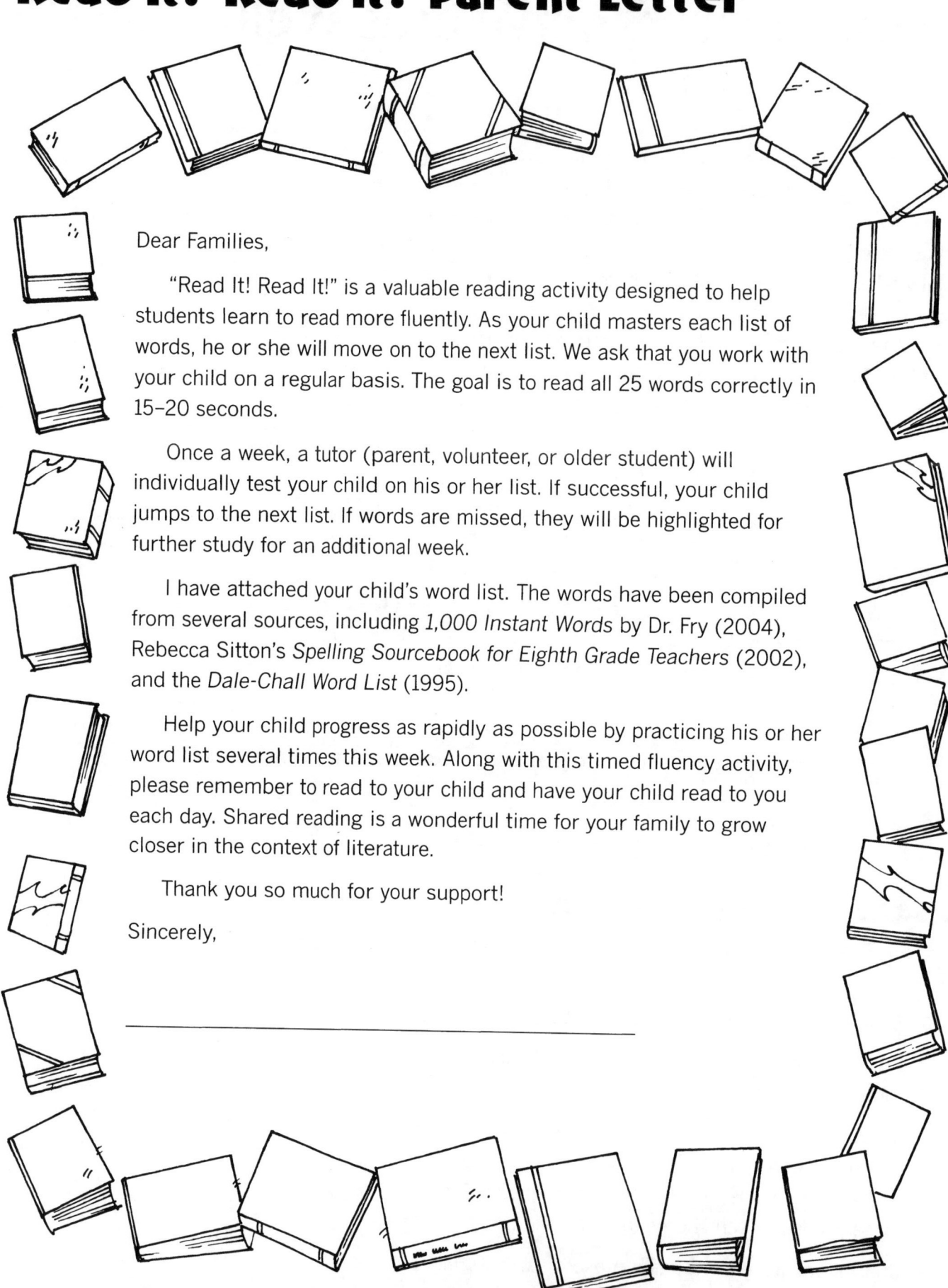

Dear Families,

"Read It! Read It!" is a valuable reading activity designed to help students learn to read more fluently. As your child masters each list of words, he or she will move on to the next list. We ask that you work with your child on a regular basis. The goal is to read all 25 words correctly in 15–20 seconds.

Once a week, a tutor (parent, volunteer, or older student) will individually test your child on his or her list. If successful, your child jumps to the next list. If words are missed, they will be highlighted for further study for an additional week.

I have attached your child's word list. The words have been compiled from several sources, including *1,000 Instant Words* by Dr. Fry (2004), Rebecca Sitton's *Spelling Sourcebook for Eighth Grade Teachers* (2002), and the *Dale-Chall Word List* (1995).

Help your child progress as rapidly as possible by practicing his or her word list several times this week. Along with this timed fluency activity, please remember to read to your child and have your child read to you each day. Shared reading is a wonderful time for your family to grow closer in the context of literature.

Thank you so much for your support!

Sincerely,

_____

Level 4 Sight Word List

List 1 garbage unable idea held didn't mild finish area sir devote kind draw I'm city law receive nick vanilla labor mean begin eleven magician answer sort

List 2 gnaw elevate women half barber course ice mind scamper ideal bald grade stood fierce quake wind real jail anything early icicle define unbeaten zone quack

List 3 habit saddle herself rainy paper abuse yearn behind hurdle great body weed return yardstick intend officer marry before usually strip public flap happiness short scene

List 4 learned decrease began above sometimes napkin pardon feed zero winter yawn consider odor perhaps different kindle import company later several racket twelve gasoline land fourth

List 5 kayak minute told among heart bail I'm American oasis nylon hatch rapid zipper line result pajamas ebony ridge appear large though ginger side increase wait

List 6 hour charge backward hair outside teacher possible jest reason condition magazine lame interest without upon swim price canyon rainbow maze lag lost passage thief start

List 7 chair navy rage hamburger youth close incline month throne jag tomorrow even knight feet equator children however babble war turn space front maple knew unequal

List 8 human fear imagination built badge garden advertise figure actor gently yard dawn sick money tangle cause picture turned enough often verb morning faithful past jeep

List 9 evening ground against court celebrate lady believe point elect scream unless office state wife cousin bacon guess fight vacation shown being least wrong miss road

List 10 fast surface become power mayor government nothing church notice educate obtain edition edit valve business word learn fiddle mane twenty kept demand father pare waffle

List 11 window rail germ whether weight whom father national won't fire wear ease change thousand kennel mark English gem carriage lard marsh air vent fifth spring

List 12 world aloud pasture stand meet language farm frolic remember absent taught damp few frequent ore either rest hundred moment damp probably lung United States murmur quarrel

List 13 really canal doctor sample fact letter service gladden brought weather strong candid speak became daily thimble catcher patch jerk wage order uncertain happen group

List 14 seen brother cost snow country anger wrote carol common less justice savage damage precious patter piece sea inspect quart remain spell cry bird music abbot

List 15 living husband dark keen oar study face matter table iceberg dairy river town during score gallop between can't move tried marriage uneven harbor darling safety

Name _____ Date _____

Level 5 Sight Word List

List 1 majority listen design break jeer effect bandage obscure particular crowd vertical quiet habitation lace debate caught ability heat objection burning unbend explain goal baby glass

List 2 decision partner native accuse machine beacon eaves smiled vault factors waiter section instead girl coast east impossible care cook son flow ears satellite fireworks tidal

List 3 tiny enclose umpire entered fault immediate listed brown game majesty melody engine length canvas Africa daylight shouted capture present scale check rolled bring correct angle

List 4 halo report sacrifice talkative electronic implore team lake trouble realize fly talent education bemoan harp natural benefit occupy fender hatchet bathroom England agony undaunted pounds

List 5 amount week suggested figure alternate cloud hat decide finally soil hole nectar cargo accomplish beautiful jiffy alone plains visit gauge dress paddle fun empire ball

List 6 affection capsule save row keeper rock earrings impatient wire rise stone thick outside business symbols bit glare God yourself surprise phrase halfway adjust bad everyone

List 7 tone travel clean legend grew major glimpse single exactly shell unaware famous mountain pants obedient gang although law property vacuum lance fall elaborate deep gas

List 8 sausage method hope cross lever dainty silent salmon past tube maybe sleep pantry address friend nation seem bargain league pavement thin provide fancy niece

List 9 thus cool tall recite joined practice fatal allege circle case teamwork happy lair drawing lot French type deflect margin period festival problem vanish killed navigate

List 10 century plan scandalize latitude tablet sent dry let's observe warm wail hill gloom speed pay blue jagged venison straight village you're gone gait iron poem

List 11 kernel expect active racer leave longer ravenous square scarf jaunt panther energy various cactus effort label copy decorate teaspoon genius mask heavy glacier keynote jealous

List 12 laundry career ultimate round kindness count data moon barrier tendril everything grass continued receipt electric varnish within bright per pushed child baggage illustrate desert metal

List 13 impression couldn't haggard tackle else indicate janitor statement earliest cadet ask compare galley oatmeal waist buy blood grasp bird trade weave insects saving beady nasty

List 14 weapon bell scarce hit paste peasant final indignant manner middle corner uncommon measure tender died emergency flat base absence manage fade carnation position free fathom

List 15 wander wafer material consonant bridge refer floor dinner wade tame whole lead smell spread regale spent sell key rich naturalist diverge fill fanciful I've wicker

Name _____ Date _____

Level 6 Sight Word List

List 1 wash dead packet busy initial note agonize race love bewilder industry wouldn't carat southern truck wasn't haunt win pair crucial measles juvenile born banquet vibrant

List 2 think humane delegate tied buffet sculptor carnival Japanese incubator matron parchment direction gasket action workers Greek drench prepared wallow imitate rind suffix difficult France arm

List 3 tango desperation tail gray sharp we'll oxygen amber string whiskers script silver habitual similar plural tense ravine seam insolvent fantastic fascinate exhibit veneer horrify march

List 4 friar hexagon division rhythm etch extricate anyone edge laboratory textile massive sage rampart seven sense defiant repeated decade gouge animate equal luster faucet chief south

List 5 conceited test immaculate havoc barbaric imprint terms gallon jargon wheedle centralized settled editorial rope beseech obligation region afraid abound becalmed quell upraise therefore unpalatable terrace

List 6 ring salad rogue agreed torment velocity malice oracle Washington parole thrive scald adjective desolate emboss located soft bayou admiration movement belong jubilant subject you'll gala

List 7 sold west martial cotton score shape create stretched flaunt salvage unstrung narrate radium judicious led finale buoy marrow doesn't fresh arrived edifice pick patent death

List 8 exciting drive lattice experience allow gesture gallery lathe branches deal seat sugar notorious thresh quaint gun cows wings western rater reservoir pretty eliminate skin wallop

List 9 fruit kitchen sedate he's inflate determine generous safe grown flounder rabble wall mine imperious contain ancestry ahead vague especially basic canopy zenith barometric diligent bad

List 10 unit match hope current northern yellow actually compound apparatus elevator nasal ventilate isn't lament chart sister jealousy describe entire board island utter ration return interesting

List 11 total heiress radio beyond grotesque hamlet hold obstacle palsy disaster freight peat keel expectant encounter inch hamper magnificent elapse niche incur stream radiator fertilizer abbreviation

List 12 yacht lavish sapling valor planets harvest soldiers pattern resign rule level inferior corn science knave fit allies census column opposite details faculties British molecules effect

List 13 product sight scrimmage nor sheep solution indignantly pull rose factories triangle send eight vivacious bought modern shop nose episode imposter track huge hit sign forward

List 14 nauseate obscene block record tools capital gnarled teeth apple reluctant pacify vagabond waver hearth operetta manifest capsize substances scanty please printed scepter patience adaptation sit

List 15 period waddle centrifugal dialog I'd laggard thaw dollars cinch necessary accentuate quartet shoulder jaunty pole value park ancient fraught scaffold forest bauble mosaic bones blow

CHAPTER 2

Read a Lot

Just reading at school is never enough. Students must read voraciously, voluminously, and voluntarily outside of school as well (Shefelbine, 1999). We need to put books in students' hands every day. One method of making sure students have books readily available is to build an extensive classroom library. Reading many books of the same genre, with familiar plotlines and vocabulary, can help build fluency.

Books in Boxes: Building an Extensive Classroom Library

A well-stocked classroom library is an essential element in any classroom. When students are surrounded by an array of interesting, magical, captivating books, they will be inspired to read. Books in boxes makes it easy for students to find a book that matches their interests. By collecting engaging used books, teachers can create a library of one thousand books or more very inexpensively.

1. Establish a classroom library by purchasing clean, good quality books at low cost from garage sales, library sales, rummage sales, thrift stores, and book clubs. Many families will also donate their old books.

2. Organize books into categories (e.g., sports, animals) and place them in plastic tubs. Books can also be boxed by author or series (e.g., Judy Blume, Roald Dahl, Scott O'Dell).

3. Label and draw a picture on the front of each box that represents the category.

4. Select a sticker for each box. Place the sticker on the outside of each box and on each book in that category so students can replace the book in the correct box by matching the stickers.

5. Make a classroom library chart that has one library card pocket with each student's name.

6. Students will write the titles of the books checked out on an index card in their library card pocket. Tell students that they must return one book before selecting another.

CHAPTER 3

Model Good Oral Reading

Read-Alouds (Grades 4–8)

Students must hear good oral reading in order to understand what fluent reading sounds like. According to Jim Trelease, "Almost as big a mistake as not reading to children at all is stopping too soon" (2006). With the crowded curriculum in older grades, reading aloud sometimes seems to be a frivolous luxury. We forget what a powerful commercial it is for the pleasures of reading and how much it assists with modeling fluent reading. In addition, reading aloud provides a number of other important benefits. It allows students to see reading as emotionally powerful, motivates them to read more, exposes them to multiple genres, and assists them in exploring sophisticated words and text structures (Rasinski, 2003). Below are some strategies you can use when reading aloud.

Before Reading the Story

1. Search the Internet for recommended read-aloud books for your grade level.

2. Select books that are at or above students' independent reading level but are on their emotional and developmental level.

3. Select a personal favorite so you can demonstrate your enthusiasm for the book.

4. Discuss reasons for selecting this particular book.

5. Introduce the book. Point out the title, author, and front and back cover illustrations.

6. Invite plausible predictions about the book.

7. Ask for possible text-to-self and text-to-text connections.

8. Discuss things students can watch or listen for during the story.

During the Story

1. Read only one chapter and allow students to decide if they want to continue with that particular book. Be flexible; if it's not working, try another book.

2. Monitor the class. Watch students' body language to become aware of signs of boredom or confusion.

978-1-4129-5828-8

3. Use enthusiasm and expression to make the story more interesting and understandable.

4. As you read, occasionally articulate aloud what is going on inside your head by saying: *You know, I was just thinking that . . .* Invite students to do the same.

5. Assist students in visualizing the story. Reread a part that lends itself to visualization. Discuss visualization as a strategy that good readers use as they imagine what is being described in the story.

When the Story Is Finished

1. Confirm or revise predictions about the story based on what was just read.

2. Ask a few questions about the story. Some examples might include: *How did this story make you feel? Has something like this ever happened to you? Does this story remind you of another book you have read?*

Teacher Modeling and Repeated Reading (Grades 4–8)

Teacher modeling and repeated reading (TMRR) works well in small reading groups with students working at the same reading level.

1. Select and copy reading passages of approximately 200 words at each student's instructional level. See the **Modeling/Repeated Reading passages (pages 17–21)**.

2. First, have students orally read their selected passage to you or a partner for one minute and then determine the number of correct words read.

3. Have them record the number of words read correctly per minute.

4. Students then read along silently while listening to an audiotape of the passage that models correct expression and phrasing, or you can model fluent reading in lieu of the audiotape.

5. Using a one-minute timer or a stopwatch, students then repeatedly read the passage until they are able to read it at a predetermined goal rate.

6. Students again read their selected passage orally to you or a partner for one minute and then determine the number of correct words read.

7. Students graph the number of words read correctly before practicing and words read correctly during the final testing.

Modeling/Repeated Reading

Newborn Island

   On a November morning nearly fifty years ago, an island was born. It is (14)
called Surtsey. It rose off the south coast of Iceland. It started six months earlier (29)
at the bottom of the sea when a volcano oozed hot lava and gas. It grew and (46)
grew. Finally, the little island poked above the waves. For awhile it grew quietly. (60)
Then it began to rumble. Explosions followed. Dark clouds of ash and steam shot (74)
hundreds of feet into the air. There was even hail and lightning. A new opening (89)
surfaced. Surtsey was then quiet for more than a year. (99)

   Then an eruption began again with a steady flow of lava that added new land (114)
to the south side of the island. By the time Surtsey was a year old, it was about (132)
one square mile in size. Once all volcanic activity stopped, the highest point on (146)
the island was more than five hundred feet above sea level. The island birth had (161)
lasted a little less than four years. (168)

   Since then the land has settled, so it is a few feet lower than it was. Surtsey (185)
is a special island. Scientists think of it as a living laboratory. They have studied (200)
it for many years. It was made into a nature reserve in 1965. (213)

Words Correct Per Minute: _____

4

Modeling/Repeated Reading

Geysers

If you watch a teakettle boil, you'll get a basic idea of how a geyser works. A (17)
geyser is a spray of steam that erupts from an opening in the earth's surface. (32)

First, a mass of magma rises to within two or three miles of the earth's (47)
surface. It heats the rock layers above. This creates a hot spot. Next, (60)
groundwater seeps deep into the heated ground. The water may reach (71)
temperatures of five hundred degrees or more. The water begins to rise (83)
through the rock. (86)

The water may surface from the earth as a hot spring or a bubbling pool of (102)
hot mud. If the super hot water fills an underground pocket, it collects there. (116)
Because it is close to the surface, the water boils, producing steam. Pressure (129)
builds up until the steam blasts the water out. The geyser erupts with a roar (144)
until the pressure is released. Then the underground pocket fills with water (156)
again, and the steam begins to build up again. (165)

The process may repeat over and over. Some geysers erupt fairly regularly. (177)
Old Faithful, in Wyoming, erupts about every seventy minutes. For up to five (190)
minutes, Old Faithful shoots out as much as twelve thousand gallons of hot water (204)
and steam. The spray rockets nearly two hundred feet high. In some places, (217)
geyser power may be harnessed as a form of clean energy. (228)

Words Correct Per Minute: _____

5

Modeling/Repeated Reading

The Gulf Stream

The Gulf Stream is one of the world's most powerful ocean currents. It forms the (15)
western boundary of a large ring of currents with a calmer region at its center. The Gulf (32)
Stream moves up to five billion cubic feet of water per second. The average bathtub (47)
only holds about three cubic feet of water. Currents are a little like streams in the (63)
ocean. They develop partly because of landforms they pass and the way ocean water (77)
is shifted by tides. Steady, global winds set up surface currents. (88)

The Gulf Stream is a system of currents joined together. It begins in the warm (103)
waters near Florida. The current rushes between islands there at about four miles per (117)
hour and up to ten miles per hour at its center. It carries one hundred times the flow of (136)
all the rivers of the world combined. When the Gulf Stream reaches the Atlantic Ocean, (151)
another current joins it. It flows north along the coast to Canada, where it becomes (166)
part of a bigger current flowing east. When it meets colder water from the Arctic, (181)
great banks of fog form. Its warm waters reach England, raising temperatures there (194)
by several degrees. After giving up its warmth, the current sinks and flows south. (208)

Words Correct Per Minute: _____

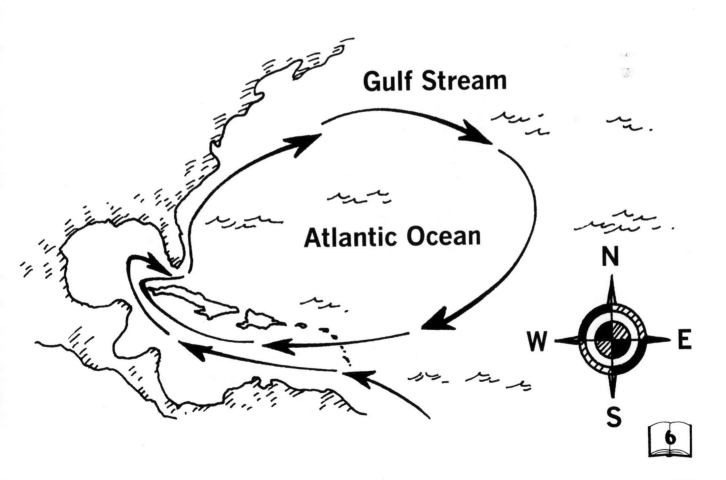

Modeling/Repeated Reading

Adventurous Dining

Every year, in an area of northeast Nigeria, swarms of ravenous locusts damage (13)
local crops and vegetation. In this desert area the losses can be devastating. The clever (28)
Nigerians have found a way to defeat the attacking locusts. They eat them! They eat (43)
the locusts, a form of grasshopper, at an annual banquet. They've even given the dish (58)
a pleasant name: desert shrimp. (63)

On almost every continent you can find a menu that includes some kind of insect. It (79)
might include beetles, ants, grasshoppers, or cockroaches. Scorpions and spiders can (90)
end up as a deep-fried snack, too. In one Asian country, giant spiders are a delicacy. (107)
They are supposed to taste best when barbecued with garlic. The tastiest part is said to (123)
be the crunchy legs. Caterpillars may be boiled or sun-dried and eaten as a treat that (140)
is high in protein. (144)

Throughout the world people regularly eat such things as guinea pigs, iguanas, rats, (157)
bats, snakes, jellyfish, and whale blubber. Certain foods are meant to be eaten raw, (171)
while others are considered ready when they are spoiled or rotten. Unusual drinks are (185)
also available for adventurous diners, such as yak tea with butter. A popular drink in (200)
Japan is sake fermented with the poison of a particular snake. (211)

Words Correct Per Minute: _____

7

Modeling/Repeated Reading

Wigs

A wig is a covering of genuine or synthetic hair worn on the head. The term *wig*, (17)
which entered the language in the late seventeenth century, is short for *periwig*, a (31)
fashionable item worn by men. Women have also worn wigs for centuries. Ancient (44)
peoples from many cultures often wore wigs to protect their heads from the sun. Wigs (59)
first became popular in Europe in the sixteenth century. Wigs had a practical function, (73)
because in those days head lice were widespread for poor and rich alike, and they were (89)
difficult to get rid of once a person was infected. The solution to lice was to shave one's (107)
head and wear a wig in public. Then, before bed, the owner could effortlessly remove (122)
the hair and the insects. (127)

In the eighteenth century, powdered wigs came into fashion. Some were extremely (139)
elaborate. Premium wigs were made of human hair, while horsehair was often employed (152)
to make less expensive wigs. The white powder was fine starch scented with flowers. (166)
Although the powdered wig fashion lasted for quite some time, the wigs were messy, (180)
uncomfortable, and inconvenient. A tax on hair powder finally brought the fad to an end. (195)

Today, wigs are as popular as ever and may be worn as a fashion choice, as a (212)
necessity, or for cultural or religious reasons. You'll rarely see a powdered wig, although (226)
actors and models wear costume wigs as part of portraying different characters. (238)

Words Correct Per Minute: _____

CHAPTER 4

Provide Oral Support for Readers

The Neurological Impress Method (Grades 4-6)

The neurological impress method (NIM) was originally used after World War II to teach brain-damaged adults to read again. NIM was first described in 1969 by Heckelman. This method can build confidence in the highly dysfluent reader (Heckelman, 1969). You can implement this strategy with students or use a tutor to help (parent volunteer, older student, or paraprofessional).

1. Select an appropriate passage for the student to read. Interest is everything, so it is extremely helpful if the topic of the book or passage is of high interest to the student.

2. Sit next to the student, so you can read into his or her ear. (Some practitioners of NIM recommend sitting nearest the ear that corresponds to the hand with which the student writes or eats.)

3. Read in unison with the student, with your speed slightly exceeding the student's normal rate. This way, the student is forced to pay attention to whole words and sentences to keep up with you.

4. Track the words by running a forefinger under them while you are reading.

5. After several joint oral readings of the text, allow the student to begin leading the reading while you maintain a secondary voice, supporting the oral reading.

6. Gradually give over the tracking responsibility to the student after repeated readings of the same text.

7. When a specific passage can be read at the selected target rate (usually a minimum of 85 words correct per minute), select a new, slightly more difficult passage.

Choral Reading (Grades 4-8)

How many of us remember a poem or a short speech that we memorized as young students? Although choral reading does not require memorization, it offers a wonderful chance for students to become familiar with some of the poetry and passages that are part of our heritage. Choral reading is especially valuable for dysfluent students, because they can have experience with more challenging text without the risk of embarrassment that often comes with solo reading.

1. Select an appropriate passage of 100–200 words (a poem, a famous speech, or an interesting passage), or use one of the **Choral Reading passages (pages 24–28)**.

2. Display the passage on an overhead projector or a chart. Or, provide one copy of the passage for each student.

3. Model the selected choral reading passage by reading it aloud to students.

4. Invite small groups or the entire class to read the text aloud together in unison.

5. Provide time for students to read selected passages repeatedly over several days until fluency, expression, and diction are near perfect.

6. If you wish, invite a guest to hear students perform or schedule small groups of students to perform for other classes.

The golden age of hip-hop mixed East and West Coast sound. Now the reach of the music is global. It's heard the world around.

Choral Reading

Soccer Then and Now

Hundreds of years in the past,
Imagine if you can.
There were playing fields in China.
Players kicked at a ball in Japan.

The Greeks had a soccer-like game.
We know that the Romans had teams.
There were lots of men on a side.
Up to twenty-seven it seems.

The modern sport of soccer
Was born in the British Isles.
The people loved the new game.
To see it they'd walk for miles.

In medieval times whole towns
Would play from breakfast to lunch.
"No hands on the ball" was the rule,
But it was okay to bite and to punch.

The king didn't seem to like it.
In fact, the sport was banned.
He thought the game was too violent,
But the people ignored his command.

Then, along came Eaton College
To establish a new set of rules.
They called the new game "football."
It was played in polite English schools.

British traders, and sailors, and soldiers
Brought the sport to other lands.
It was played in northern countries,
And in the south it was in demand.

When played in the U S of A,
Soccer was its name.
At first very few seemed to like it.
It wasn't a popular game.

Then in the 1930s,
The U.S. was in the World Cup.
We got there again in the sixties,
And support of soccer went up.

Now millions of kids play soccer.
You can bet they'll never forget
How it feels to go for the goal
And kick the ball into the net.

Reproducible 978-1-4129-5828-8 • © Corwin Press

Choral Reading

When I'm Grown

I can't imagine what I'll be
When I become full-grown.
There are lots of things I'd like to do
When I'm on my own.

I could be a surgeon,
Or maybe I'll be a vet.
I might like to be a lawyer.
I haven't decided yet.

Perhaps I'll be an artist.
I'd have to learn to draw.
I'd paint great masterpieces
Without mistakes or flaws.

There's always entertainment.
I could be a star.
If I danced, or sang, or acted,
I know I could go far.

Racecars could be exciting.
I'd drive at amazing speed.
Everything sounds inviting,
And I'm growing like a weed.

Maybe I'll be an athlete.
I could play softball,
Or hockey or soccer or tennis.
I really like them all.

How about being a chef?
I know I could take the heat.
I think I'd be just perfect.
I certainly like to eat.

This thinking is making me dizzy.
Who knows what I'll be
When I become the grown-up me?
For now I'm just glad to be ten.

5

Choral Reading

Friends

Group 1: Why is it important for a person to have a friend?
Group 2: A person needs someone on whom they can depend.

Group 1: What makes a friendship last between a special pair?
Group 2: Good friends have things in common, things that they can share.

Group 1: What is one special trait in friendship that's a must?
Group 2: A caring and true friend is one that you can trust.

Group 1: Name another thing that good friends always do.
Group 2: When you have a problēm, friends help you think it through.

Group 1: What is an important part of friendship one cannot buy?
Group 2: The way a friend can make you laugh when you want to cry.

Group 1: What is a special way to show a friend you care?
Group 2: When a friend reaches out to you, let him know you're there.

Group 1: What's the worth of friendship? How much is its measure?
Group 2: A good friendship is precious. It's as priceless as a treasure.

Choral Reading

The House Next Door

Just about a week ago, new neighbors moved next door.
They moved into the mansion, the one that has three floors.
They pulled up to the rusting gates ten minutes to midnight.
I saw them from my window. They were an awful sight.

The dad was nearly eight feet tall. His skin was scaly blue.
The mom had long and pointy fangs. The children had them, too.
There was a boy about my age; his eyes were blazing red.
There was one girl or maybe two; her body had two heads.

I thought they had a great big dog. I thought its tail was waggin'.
But when I got a closer look, I saw it was a dragon.
It breathed two spheres of flickering flame out from where its nose is.
Its breath destroyed our privet hedge and barbecued Mom's roses.

They parked their car. It was a hearse painted shiny black.
The seats were lined with satin with a coffin in the back.
The boy held up a darkened cage. Inside, there was a bird.
When the family lumbered to the porch, it didn't say a word.

It was a raven, I could see, as they got to the door.
And when the father turned the key, the bird said, "Nevermore."
The luggage left beside the car let out a mournful moan.
When no one came to pick it up, it walked in on its own.

The second night their furniture arrived in two large vans.
In the first were brooms and chains and several music stands.
The second truck revealed a pair of keyboards and a fiddle.
Guitars galore, and tambourines, and a drum set in the middle.

Turns out the neighbors love to rock, and music is their passion.
So who am I to criticize their quirky kind of fashion?
The mom plays on the keyboards, but little sister's torn.
One head likes to play the flute; the other likes French horn.

The dragon plays the tambourine. He shakes it with his tail.
And on the drums dad does his thing. Man, that guy can wail.
Brother plays a mean guitar, so I thought, "What the heck?"
I joined the band. I play the bass, with garlic 'round my neck.

Choral Reading

All About Music

In a house on Sedgwick Avenue,
They say hip-hop was born
In the west Bronx of New York,
In a high-rise old and worn.

The music emerged in the seventies.
Called disco rap, it thrived.
Then Keith Cowboy named it hip-hop.
He sang with Furious Five.

The golden age of hip-hop
Mixed East and West Coast sound.
Now the reach of the music is global.
It's heard the world around.

Rock music has its roots
In fifties rock and roll.
It blended folk and country.
It added a touch of soul.

Chuck Berry and Bo Diddley
Were among the early rockers.
They were followed by Bill Haley
And other rock-around-the-clockers.

Buddy Holly and Big Bopper
Were of the rock persuasion.
Then Elvis was the king,
Until the British invasion.

Now rock has many faces
There's soft rock, blues rock, and funk.
There's metal and techno and indie
And grunge rock, hard rock, and punk.

There are many styles of music
For everyone to choose.
There's jazz, pop, and classical,
Latin, country, and blues.

No matter what you listen to
Or who's in your music crowd,
Enjoy your music often
And turn the volume loud.

8

Fluency Development (Grades 4-8)

The fluency development lesson is a combination of reading aloud, choral reading, listening to students read, and reading performance. This lesson should be implemented on a daily basis, for several weeks, but need not take longer than 15 minutes each day (Rasinski, 2003).

For this exercise, select short, predictable passages of 150–200 words, such as the **Fluency Development passages (pages 30–34)**. Poetry from the Choral Reading passages (pages 24–28) and Modeling/Repeated Reading passages (pages 17–21) are excellent to use for this exercise as well. Students will also enjoy selecting their own poetry and short stories from the classroom library for fluency development.

1. Make one copy of the passage for each student or place a copy of the passage on an overhead projector.

2. Model reading the passage aloud, using a variety of voices, including a dysfluent, unexpressive voice.

3. Next, briefly discuss students' perceptions of the different voices and why the unexpressive, staccato voice is unpleasant.

4. Then, as students listen, fluently read the passage aloud.

5. Briefly discuss the meaning of the passage and identify any difficult vocabulary.

6. Have students work in pairs. Ask partners to read the passage at least three times to each other.

7. Have partners provide feedback, assistance, and support.

8. Partners can then perform for an interested audience.

Fluency Development

Blue Moon

Have you ever heard someone say something happens "once in a blue moon"? What they mean is that something is rare. It happens once in a while but not often. So what does that have to do with the moon?

Actually, there are two definitions for a blue moon. The older one relates to the seasons. There are four seasons in each year: spring, summer, fall, and winter. Each season usually has three full moons. That makes twelve full moons annually. Every once in a while, there are thirteen full moons per year instead of twelve. That means that one of the seasons had four full moons instead of three. The extra moon is a blue moon.

The modern definition is the second full moon in a month. The moon travels around the earth every 29.5 days. Usually there is only one full moon in that time. If the first one occurs at the very beginning of the month, it's possible to squeeze in one more full moon at the end of the month. The extra full moon is called a blue moon. The only time this cannot happen is in February. Can you figure out why?

A blue moon really isn't as rare as people think. In the next twenty years there will be about seventeen blue moons, and that will be about evenly divided between the old version and the modern version. What is rare is to have two blue moons in the same year. This happens about once every twenty years. Double blue moons usually occur in January and March. Do you know why that is? Think about it, because puzzles like this only come along once in a blue moon!

4

Fluency Development

A Great Explorer

Roy Chapman Andrews was a real dinosaur hunter. He was born in 1884. Even as a child, he wanted to be an explorer. He spent lots of time exploring the woods near his home. Part of his dream was to work for a museum.

One month after he graduated from college, Andrews went to New York to find a job. The only position open at the museum was as a janitor. Andrews took the job. He was willing to do anything, including scrub floors. He worked hard and learned as much as he could. Within two years, he earned a spot on an expedition. He went to the East Indies to collect snakes and lizards.

By 1920, Andrews led his own expedition to Mongolia. The group searched in the Gobi Desert. They had to put up with heat, sandstorms, and bandits. The explorers found lots of fossils and discovered new kinds of dinosaurs. They were the first ever to discover dinosaur eggs and nests.

After many years of scientific exploration, Andrews became the director of the museum. In 1941, he retired to his country home. Andrews spent much of his time writing. He even wrote books about dinosaurs for children. When Andrews passed away in 1960, scientists around the world agreed that he was one of the greatest naturalists of the twentieth century.

Mongolia

Gobi Desert

5

Fluency Development

The Pony Express

Starting on April 3, 1860, the Pony Express delivered mail from Missouri to California. The route was about two thousand miles long. It passed through eight present-day states. There were about two hundred riders in all. Most of them weighed a little more than one hundred pounds and were about twenty to thirty years old. The youngest was eleven.

Mail carriers rode day and night, every day. On an average day, a rider covered up to one hundred miles. He changed horses at special stations that were about ten or fifteen miles apart. In one leap the rider transferred himself and his mochila to a fresh horse. The *mochila* was a special saddle cover that had four pockets for the mail.

The first delivery by Pony Express took about ten days. Mail delivered by stagecoach took twice as long. Packages sent by boat could take months to reach their destination. The fastest Pony Express delivery was in 1861. Riders carried the President's inaugural address to the West Coast in less than eight days.

At first, the Pony Express was a private business. For six months it operated under contract as a government mail route. When telegraph lines finally spanned the nation, the Pony Express was no longer needed. Although it had run for only about eighteen months, the Pony Express became a legend.

6

Fluency Development

Summer Vacation

Most schools in the United States operate on a schedule of nine months in class and three months off. The three-month break usually takes place from June to September and is known as the summer vacation. This system is unique in the world. Children in most other industrialized countries spend more hours per day and more days per year in school.

The long summer vacation hasn't always been customary in the United States. Rural schools in the 1800s often took two shorter breaks. Farm families counted on children to help with planting in the spring and harvesting in the fall. The school year had to be scheduled from December to March and from May to August. In large cities, children often went to school for eleven months per year.

Families of today view the summer vacation differently. Some parents feel that the time off is important. They want to have uninterrupted time with their children to travel or enjoy recreational activities. Other parents work year-round and have a difficult time finding ways to keep their children safe and entertained during the long summer days. The solution is often a combination of summer programs, camp, or day care. Some teachers believe that a long summer break is hard on students because many return to school in September having to relearn what they forgot over vacation.

Schools are trying alternatives. Some stay in session year-round. Groups of students still take three months off, but at different times. Other schools offer multiple vacations that are shorter in length. Without a doubt, the time could come when the summer vacation is a thing of the past.

Fluency Development

The Ride of Your Life

There are traditionally two types of people—those who love roller coasters and those who cannot be persuaded to ride them under any circumstances! There are two types of roller coasters, too—steel and wooden. The tracks or rails determine which is which. Steel coasters may include wooden support structures, but the tracks are made of steel. They are known for providing a smooth ride, and the rails are more flexible so they can be twisted to generate elements such as loops, barrel rolls, wingovers, corkscrews, pretzels, and many others. A wooden roller coaster boasts tracks constructed of laminated wood with a flat steel rail on top. They do not have a smooth ride, but they are notororious for offering a lot of airtime. That is the floating sensation you experience when the G-forces of a nail-biting drop lift you out of your seat and abandon your stomach somewhere in the upper atmosphere. Wooden coasters are characteristically made up of a series of hills, called camel backs, that provide an overabundance of airtime.

Typically, passengers sit facing forward in the car, but not always. There are coasters that have the rider standing or facing backwards. Some even forgo the base and leave riders dangling in the air. The cars, or train, on both types are rarely self-powered. They are customarily pulled up the track with a chain or cable. Loaded with potential energy at the pinnacle of the lift, they speed down the other side due to the force of gravity.

In spite of the fact that some roller coasters are so scary that they can make grown men cry, they are statistically safe. You are ultimately delivered back to the starting point. Whether you decide to get back in line for another ride is up to you.

8

CHAPTER 5

Offer Plenty of Practice

Offering multiple opportunities for repeated reading practice builds reading fluency. Repeated reading practice is most enjoyable in the context of "Reading Buddies" or "Reader's Theater." First, however, it is important to carefully choose interesting passages at the appropriate readability levels so students can comfortably make incremental progress in fluency.

How to Choose Text for Repeated Oral Reading (Grades 4–8)

Choose selections of about 150–200 words that are on students' independent reading level (the highest level at which students can read without assistance, with few errors in word recognition and with good comprehension and recall). All too frequently, students are given text to read that is at their frustrational level. When students are frustrated by the difficulty of the text, reading skills break down, fluency disappears, errors in word recognition become numerous, comprehension remains faulty, recall is sketchy, and signs of emotional tension and discomfort become evident (Harris & Sipay, 1985). Older students, in particular, begin avoiding reading when they are frustrated by the process.

Time students' reading of a sample passage and note the number of correct words and the number of errors. If students take more than two minutes to read a passage or make more than five errors, the passage is too difficult. If students can read a passage at 85 words per minute with two or fewer errors, the passage is too easy. Choose a more difficult one.

If a passage is deemed suitable for repeated reading practice, go over any errors that were made. Ask students to repeatedly read the chosen passage until they are confident in their reading. Practice can take several forms, including reading orally to themselves, listening to an audiotape while reading along and then reading orally without the tape, or reading the selection orally to an adult or peer. Always take note of the words correct per minute. Teachers, aides, volunteers, or older students can graph students' progress over time on a chart. The goal is for students to improve their fluency in reading challenging material to at least 85 words correct per minute before moving on to a new passage.

Radio Reading (Grades 4–8)

For "Radio Reading," students are assigned selected portions of a text to use for shared reading, read-alouds, or lessons in content-area texts (Searfoss, 1975). "Radio Reading" works well in lieu of reading aloud to students.

1. Have small groups of students work together, practicing unison reading of the passage and focusing on expression and fluency. They can pretend to read into handmade microphones if they wish.

2. More proficient students can read parts of the chapter solo.

3. Assign an "announcer," who reads the opening and closing portions of the passage or chapter and introduces the guest "radio readers."

Read Around (Grades 4–8)

"Read Around" provides an easy method for motivating students to read a passage of their own choosing until it is polished for a quick performance (Tompkins, 1998). "Read Around" can be a required activity or offered as an optional opportunity for students once or twice a week.

1. Invite students to choose a favorite poem, narrative text, or lyrics, or use the **Read Around passages (pages 37–41)**.

2. Have students rehearse the passage until they can read it fluently.

3. Students then read the passage to peers, a small group, or the entire class.

Read Around

Water

I am the ocean.
Look and you will see
Whale and shark and tuna
Swimming wild and free.

I am a lake,
So deep my waters flow.
Ducks nest on my shoreline
Where the cattails grow.

I am a river.
Tumbling from my source,
My nature changes often
As I travel along my course.

I am a pond.
I'm home to dragonflies,
Turtles, snails, and tadpoles.
A muskrat lives nearby.

I am a swamp.
My water's dark and low.
Animals abound here
Where the cypress grow.

I am a bay.
Land is on three sides of me.
My waters are a haven
When storms are out at sea.

I am a canal,
An inland waterway.
I'm dug to bring fresh water
Where people work and play.

I am a channel.
I often connect two seas.
Mighty ships will cross me
If I'm deep and hazard free.

I am a marsh.
I'm a shallow changing blend
Of fresh and salty water
Where the shorelines end.

4

Read Around

The Skunk

If you make a list of animals
Who truly grip your heart,
It isn't very likely
Skunk will be a part.

But if you take some time
To reflect upon your choice,
You might reconsider
If skunk just had a voice.

He'd tell you he's a mammal
From a long, impressive line.
His ancestors were here
Well before yours and mine.

Oftentimes we humans
Dress without a care.
But skunk is always decked out
In black-tie formal wear.

Skunk's defense is smelly,
Everyone agrees.
But it isn't always used.
It's limited, you see.

Skunk can only spray
A few times in ten days.
So when skunk feels threatened,
He'd rather run away.

Skunk has a bushy tail
And short legs with clawed feet.
He has sharp teeth to chomp
All the things he likes to eat.

Skunk eats worms and eggs
And fruit and plants and fish.
Skunk thinks that rodents
Are a very tasty dish.

Skunk eats harmful insects,
So if he's near your home,
Remember he has a purpose
And leave the skunk alone.

5

Read Around

Hobbies

My father plays with yo-yos.
My mother likes them, too.
Grandpa Alfred was a yo-yo champ
In nineteen fifty-two.

Grandma Violet loves her hula-hoop.
You should see it spin.
She twirls it round three times a day.
She says it keeps her slim.

My Auntie Jane can spend all day
With a crossword in her lap.
What's a four-word clue for *snare*?
I think the word is *trap*.

Uncle Cedric likes a challenge.
Jigsaw is his game.
Those puzzles make me crazy.
The parts all look the same.

My cousin likes adventure.
I think she is insane.
She's training now to meet her goal
Of jumping from a plane.

My best friend loves his music.
I know he will go far.
His leisure time is always spent
Strumming his guitar.

At school I play some soccer.
I also like to cook.
But when it comes to hobbies,
I love to read a book.

Read Around

A Work of Art

I sit before a formless lump of clay.
My teacher instructs me to mold it.
But what should I do?

The clay is supple in my hands.
There are unlimited choices.
But what can I do?

The future stretches out before me.
It offers so much.
But what must I do?

I take the clay in my hands;
Its ultimate form is up to me.
But what will I do?

I begin to make a shape.
The lines change as I work.
But I know what to do.

My friends try to tell me
The form that I should make.
But must I conform?

My parents try to tell me
The way the form should be.
But can't I make my own choice?

My heart leads my work.
The clay takes shape.
But will it be true?

The clay moves beneath my hands
But remains fluid and flexible.
The future remains to be seen.

7

Read Around

Lifelong Friends

Sweet and gentle little life,
A puppy newly born.
To this tiny furry angel
My heart is quickly sworn.

Little critter, clumsy still,
With a tumble and a roll.
She gets back up and runs again,
A chew toy is her goal.

We both grow tall and strong.
She runs just like the wind.
But when she hears my beckoning call,
She comes right back again.

Through thick and thin we're buddies.
She always wants to play.
If I'm busy doing homework,
She'll try another day.

The years have made her noble.
She stands with quiet grace.
No matter what the world may bring,
My side is still her place.

Of late she seems to nap a lot.
I watch her sleeping there.
As long as she can feel me near,
She doesn't have a care.

The day will come, I know it's true,
When we will have to part.
But she has claimed me for all time,
For her pawprint's on my heart.

Reading Buddies (Grades 4-6)

Older readers, who may be reluctant to engage in enough repeated oral readings of grade-level text to develop fluency, will usually jump at the chance to read aloud to younger students. Teachers can arrange "reading buddy" partnerships between two classrooms. Students in the older classroom can be assigned to younger students who will be their regular reading buddies throughout the year. Older students visit the younger students' classroom and read books to their young friends.

1. In preparation for their read-aloud sessions, have older readers select high-interest books appropriate for younger students. Then ask them to engage in several repeated readings of their books without an audience.

2. Have older readers read the books aloud to as many listeners as they can find, including an adult, a parent, or a volunteer.

3. Then invite older students to read the practiced books to younger students during scheduled read-aloud sessions.

4. Debrief with older readers following each set of read-aloud sessions regarding fluency progress.

Reader's Theater (Grades 4-8)

"Reader's Theater" helps text come alive as students take on the roles presented in short plays. This method of repeated reading enables students to participate in the reading of a play without the props, scenery, and endless rehearsal. Students do not memorize lines or wear costumes. They just repeatedly read their parts orally in preparation for the performance (Opitz & Rasinski, 1998).

1. In preparation for the activity, gather tapes of old radio shows. The library and Internet are great resources.

2. Play some of the recordings and discuss how powerful text can be when read fluently and with expression.

3. Select an appropriate script from the **Reader's Theater reproducibles (pages 43-62)**. Assign each student a part in the play.

4. Have students individually and as a group practice their parts to improve their delivery. Then students can practice the play as a group.

5. Ask students to perform the play for the class or invite guests to attend their performance.

978-1-4129-5828-8

Reader's Theater

Messenger Relay

Cast of Characters: David, Logan, Armando, Haily, Andra, Sara, Miss Carter (fourth-grade teacher)

> **Scene One:** *Miss Carter's class at Condit Elementary School. Students are sitting at their desks, and Miss Carter is at the front of the room. Students are taking out their science books.*

Miss Carter: Hold on. You won't need your science books today. We're going to be spending this class time out on the playground.

David: Cool.

Haily: Great!

Miss Carter: First, I'd like you to tell me about some of your favorite playground games. Tell me what you like and why. I always liked four-square and hopscotch. Do any of you still play that?

Sara: I've never heard of four-square.

Andra: I have. Four players bounce a ball back and forth in a four-square court. I like handball better because it's fast and you have to keep moving. And I like the competition.

Armando: My favorite game is tetherball. That's fast, too. It looks easy, but it takes a lot of strategy.

Miss Carter: That's good. Anyone else?

David: Dodgeball is the best. I like it when we play in teams. You have to watch what your teammate is doing so you don't get in each other's way. It can be really fast, too, and you have to make a lot of decisions.

Logan: I like basketball, but I'm not very good at it.

Sara: You don't have to be good at it to have fun.

Logan: It helps!

Reader's Theater

Messenger Relay (cont.)
The class laughs.

Miss Carter: Okay. You all came up with some good games. Now here is what I want you to do. I want you to form groups of six. Each group will make up a new playground game.

Haily: Any kind of game?

Miss Carter: Yes, as long as it is safe. There is one other rule. It has to use science in some way. You can use materials from the classroom. When you're ready, just write the rules on notepaper. Now let's go outside.

Exit Andra, Haily, Sara, Armando, David, Logan, and Miss Carter.

> **Scene Two:** *Playground.*

Logan: Does anyone have any ideas?

Sara: We all like games that have a lot of action, and we like team sports. How about a ball game?

David: We like competition, too. Maybe we could do some kind of team sport like soccer or football.

Haily: How about a race?

Andra: We could do a relay race, but how can we use science? You can't do an experiment while you're running.

Armando: Maybe we could use a rocket to start the race.

Logan (laughing): Yeah, right. I think Miss Carter said something about the game being safe.

Sara: It doesn't have to be a rocket.

Andra: What do you mean?

Sara: Remember what we did in class last week with the balloon?

Reader's Theater

Messenger Relay (cont.)

Haily: You want to send up a balloon?

Sara: No, not send *up* a balloon . . . send it *across*.

Armando: I don't get it.

David: I do. Last week we taped a straw to a balloon and put it on a string that was tied from the door to a desk.

Logan: That's right. Then we put baking soda and vinegar in the balloon and held the opening closed. When we let go, the balloon took off across the string. It went a long way before it stopped.

Armando: Like a rocket!

Andra: I get it! We can send a message by balloon rocket.

Haily: What kind of message?

Sara: The way to move the ball. We can have two teams at the one end of the field. Each team has a ball, and a player at the other end decides how the runner has to bring the ball across the finish line. They can tape the message on the balloon and send it down a line.

Logan: I don't think the balloon will get all the way across the field.

David: It can go to another player halfway across the field, and that person can bring the message the rest of the way.

Andra: I think that's a really good idea. What are some of the ways the team can move the ball?

Logan: They could dribble it like in basketball.

Sara: Or dribble it like in soccer.

Haily: They could balance it on their head or carry it with their knees.

Reader's Theater

Messenger Relay (cont.)

Andra: Or kick it while running backwards. That would be funny.

David: I think we have plenty of ideas. Each runner will have to move the ball differently. The first team to cross the finish line wins!

Sara: The game needs a name, something that's easy to remember. What do you think we should call it?

Logan: The instructions come by special messenger, so maybe we could call it Special Delivery Relay.

Armando: Or Special Messenger Relay.

Haily: That's kind of long.

Andra: How about Messenger Relay?

Armando: That's perfect! Let's go back to the classroom and write it all down.

Exit Andra, Haily, Sara, Armando, David, and Logan.

Scene Three: *Enter class: Andra, Haily, Sara, Armando, David, and Logan. Miss Carter is at her desk. They write down their game idea and give it to Miss Carter.*

Miss Carter: Thank you. Let's see what you have come up with.

She reads the paper.

Miss Carter: This is a very good idea. I think you should all know that you have earned an A+ on your project!

David: There's only one thing better than an A+.

Sara: What's that?

David: Science class is over, and it's time for recess. Let's get everything we need and play Messenger Relay!

Reader's Theater

Pirates!

Cast of Characters: Narrator 1, Narrator 2, Mom, Maggie, Joshua, Nathaniel, Annabelle, Pirate Voice

> **Scene One:** *Maggie's bedroom. She is up late reading a book.*

Narrator 1: Maggie is in bed reading a book. Her younger brother, Joshua, is sound asleep in the next bedroom. Her mother knocks on her door.

Mom: Maggie, are you still reading?

Maggie: Yes, Mom. This book is so amazing! It's about a brother and sister who get kidnapped by pirates. It's kind of funny.

Mom: I thought your brother was the one who liked pirates. Besides, being kidnapped by pirates doesn't sound all that funny.

Maggie: It's funny because of *why* they're kidnapped. The pirates hate eating the same kind of food day after day. They want someone to cook for them. I only have a few pages left. The kids have escaped, and they just need to find a way off the island.

Mom: For now, I'd be delighted if you got some sleep. You have school tomorrow.

Maggie: Okay. Good night, Mom.

Exit Mom. Go dark.

Narrator 2: Maggie fell asleep in her own bed, but she isn't there now. She is sleeping on a sandy beach. Joshua is asleep a few feet away. Two children in old-fashioned clothes are standing over them.

Nathaniel (poking Maggie): Wake up! Wake up! It isn't safe here.

Annabelle: Look at how strangely they are dressed, Nathaniel. Where do you think they came from? Maybe they are scoundrels in league with the pirates.

Maggie (stretching): Please, Mom, can I sleep just a little bit longer?

Nathaniel: If you stay here, the pirates will discover you.

Reader's Theater

Pirates! (cont.)

Maggie (sitting up): Pirates! Who are you, and where am I?

Joshua (sitting up): Pirates?

Nathaniel: The question is, who are *you*, and how did you come to be here?

Maggie: My name is Maggie Bennett, and this is my brother Joshua. I don't know how I got here. I don't even know where *here* is.

Joshua: Wow! How cool. Look, Maggie.

Narrator 1: A large ship is in the lagoon, and it flies the Jolly Roger, the flag of pirates.

Nathaniel: You are on an island. I'm not sure which one because my sister Annabelle and I were captured by pirates when our ship was attacked. My name is Nathaniel.

Maggie: Wait a minute. This sounds familiar. Nathaniel . . . Annabelle . . . pirates?

Annabelle: Yes. They captured us and forced us to cook their meals. It has been an unbelievably terrible ordeal.

Joshua: Hey, I remember something like that. It was in a book I read.

Pirate Voice: There they are!

Annabelle: The pirates have spotted us! Run quickly so we can hide!

Nathaniel: This way! We must run toward the hills.

Joshua: No, wait! I read this book, and there was something important at the end.

Narrator 2: The pirates raced toward the children. Nathaniel led the way as they escaped through the undergrowth.

Maggie: There are so many of them! Whatever are we going to do?

Nathaniel: This way! There is a cave where we can conceal ourselves from our captors.

Annabelle: Quickly! If they capture us, we are lost.

5

Reader's Theater

Pirates! (cont.)

Narrator 1: Nathaniel led the way. They wriggled under a fallen tree and behind a bramble bush.

Narrator 2: The opening to the cave was low to the ground and difficult to see. The children crawled inside where it was dark and damp.

Nathaniel: Keep very quiet. We don't want them to hear us.

Narrator 1: The children curled up in the shadows and waited breathlessly. The pirates rushed past the opening. They beat the bushes and jabbed their swords here and there. They didn't see the children and soon disappeared.

Maggie: Do you think it's safe now?

Annabelle: I think we should stay here for a while to be sure they don't come back.

Nathaniel: Maggie, you didn't say where you were from or how you came to be here.

Maggie: I'm from a small town in the United States.

Nathaniel: I have heard of those states. I have heard of your famous president, George Washington. Were you shipwrecked?

Maggie: No, I went to sleep in my bed at home. When I woke up, I was here.

Annabelle: That sounds very strange. How do you think this came to be?

Maggie: I think I might be dreaming. I was reading a book about two children kidnapped by pirates. Their names were Nathaniel and Annabelle.

Nathaniel: I promise you, I am not a dream.

Annabelle: Maybe you have been sent to rescue us. Maybe you have been sent to help us get away from this miserable island.

Joshua: Now I remember the story! This isn't an island, it's a peninsula.

Nathaniel: Whatever do you mean?

Reader's Theater

Pirates! (cont.)

Joshua: In the story, Nathaniel and Annabelle escaped to a nearby settlement.

Annabelle: Thank you, Joshua. Will you come with us?

Maggie: I just want to go home, but I don't even understand how we got here.

Joshua: All you need to do is hike over these hills. It will be difficult, but you will make it, I promise you. You'll be back with your parents soon.

Pirate Voice: This way, mates! They must be sheltering here in these caves!

Annabelle: They're coming back, so we have to hurry!

Nathaniel: Toward the hills! Everyone run!

Narrator 2: The children scrambled out of the cave and raced toward the hills. They kept low as they ran; however, Maggie and Joshua began to go slower and slower.

Maggie: I can't run anymore. I'm so tired.

Joshua: Me, too. This grass is so soft and cozy. Maybe I'll just stop and rest for a while.

Annabelle: No, Joshua, don't stop.

Narrator 1: It was too late. Joshua was sound asleep, and Maggie curled up beside him.

Maggie: Don't worry about us. You two go on. I have a feeling we'll all be fine.

Nathaniel: Good-bye, Maggie, and thank you.

Exit Nathaniel, Annabelle, and Joshua. Enter Mom.

Narrator 2: When Maggie woke up, the sun was streaming through her bedroom window. Someone knocked on the door.

Mom: Time to wake up, Maggie. If you get ready for school fast enough, maybe you'll have enough time to finish your book.

Maggie (smiling): That's okay, Mom. I have a feeling I know how it ends.

Reader's Theater

The Ring
Cast of Characters: Demmond, Jake, Madison, Alex, Sula,
Dad, Narrator

> ***Scene One:*** *Kitchen of Demmond's house. He is working on a social studies project with his classmates, Madison, Alex, and Sula.*

Narrator: Demmond and his friends are at his house, and they are working on a school project at the kitchen table. They are making a model of a medieval village.

Demmond: This looks pretty good, but I think we should put more trees around the outside because it's supposed to be near a forest.

Sula: There are a few more in the container. I'll get them.

Alex: Maybe we should make a river at the edge of the forest, because usually villages were built near streams or rivers.

Madison: I still think that we should have made a castle. It would have been so cool to have banners, knights in armor, and horses. I would have liked to make a moat and a drawbridge.

Alex: All of the other groups are making castles. Our project will be unique. At least it will if I can figure out how to make a thatched roof for this blacksmith shop. Do we have any straw?

Demmond: I'll bet my mom has an old broom that we could take apart. That would be perfect.

Sula: What is thatch anyway?

Alex: It's the material some people used to make the roof of a building. Usually it was grass or straw, but sometimes builders used water reeds. It depended on what grew nearby. The best thing about thatched roofs, though, is that they were lighter than other kinds of roofs and not difficult to repair.

Sula: It sounds like thatched roofs would have been cold and leaky.

Demmond: I read that thatched roofs were excellent if they were constructed properly. They were bulky, but the grass or straw held up nicely in all kinds of weather. The roofs had plenty of air pockets in them. That meant they were insulated, so they were good at keeping the houses toasty in winter and cool in summer.

Alex: The roofs usually weren't leaky, but sometimes birds or rodents made nests in them. Lots of insects burrowed into them, too.

Reader's Theater

The Ring (cont.)

Madison: Yuck. I'll bet thatched roofs would have been dangerous in a fire. You wouldn't have found a thatched roof on a castle!

Enter Jake, Demmond's older brother.

Jake: Hey, Demmond, have you seen my class ring? It's the gold one with the sapphire. I had it on this morning, but now I can't find it. I think it might have slipped off my finger.

Demmond: I haven't seen it.

Madison: Have you checked the counter in the bathroom? My mom is always leaving her jewelry next to the sink when she washes her hands.

Jake: Yes, I looked by the sink in the bathroom and in the kitchen, too. I also looked on my dresser, and I checked my pockets. No luck.

Demmond: Maybe we can help you to find it.

Alex: All you have to do is think about the last time you saw it and what you did after that.

Jake: Okay. I had it on when I got dressed this morning. I had breakfast, and I remember seeing it on my finger while I was eating my cereal. Then I did my chores.

Sula: Here's a notebook and a pencil, so you can list all the chores you did after breakfast.

Narrator: Jake wrote five chores on the list. He had made his bed, sorted his laundry, put his library book in the hall to be taken back to the library, raked the front lawn, and fed his two pet hamsters.

✓ Make bed
✓ Sort laundry
✓ Library book
✓ Rake lawn
✓ Feed rats

Demmond: Let's see . . . I'll check the bedroom. Alex, why don't you look in the hallway and check those library books.

Madison: I'll poke around outside in the front yard. The ring might have fallen into the flowerbed, or it could be in the bag with the leaves.

Sula: I'll take a look in the hamster cage. My hamsters like shiny things, and I've found coins and hair clips in their cage at home. They would love jewelry, especially a ring with a glittering saphire in it.

Jake: Where should I search?

Reader's Theater

The Ring (cont.)

Demmond: How about checking the laundry basket?

Exit Demmond, Jake, Madison, Alex, and Sula.

Scene Two: *Kitchen*

Narrator: The children went to search for Jake's ring. They were gone for a while. Demmond was the first to return, and he waited until everyone was back in the kitchen before he spoke.

Enter Demmond, then Jake, Madison, Alex, and Sula.

Demmond: Did anyone find the ring?

Jake, Madison, Alex, and Sula all shake their heads "no."

Madison: I looked around in the front yard and in the flowerbeds. I checked the bag of leaves Jake raked up. I found a squeaky dog toy, but I didn't locate the ring.

Demmond: How about you, Alex?

Alex: I looked on the table in the hallway. I looked under the table, too. I even looked through the library books. I found this photograph of your basketball team, Jake. You must have been using it for a bookmark. But I didn't locate the ring.

Sula: I was sure I was going to find it in the hamster cage. I checked in the food bowl and in the bag of food next to the cage. I checked in the little house that the hamsters sleep in. I found this quarter, but I didn't locate the ring.

Jake: I looked through the laundry twice, and I found two dollar bills. But I didn't locate the ring.

Demmond: I didn't have any luck, either. I looked under your pillow and under the blankets on your bed. I searched under the bed and found the catcher's mitt you were looking for yesterday. But I didn't locate the ring.

Jake: Thanks a lot for helping me, but I can't think of anywhere else to search.

Madison: I'm sorry, Jake. Maybe it will turn up later.

Enter Dad.

Dad: Hi, kids. Why does everyone look so serious?

Reader's Theater

The Ring (cont.)

Jake: I can't find my class ring, and everyone was helping me look.

Dad: I'm sorry to hear that you can't find your ring. I understand how much you like it. Don't give up because it has to be here somewhere. In the meantime, here is a letter from your cousin, Demmond. It was with the mail on the table in the living room.

Demmond: Thanks, Dad.

Jake: Hey, wait a minute! I forgot that I brought in the mail. The ring might be on the coffee table, too. Let's go look.

Narrator: The children checked the coffee table in the living room. They looked under the couch cushions and on the floor.

Alex: It was an interesting thought, but the ring isn't here either.

Sula: I'm sorry, Jake.

Madison: We've looked everywhere.

Demmond: Not everywhere. I have an idea. Follow me.

Narrator: The children followed Demmond out onto the front porch. He opened the mailbox and reached inside.

Demmond: I feel something in the bottom of the mailbox.

Narrator: Demmond pulled out a gold ring with a sapphire.

Jake: My ring! You found it!

Madison: It must have slipped off when you got the mail.

Sula: Way to go, Demmond!

Jake: Thanks, Demmond. You're a fantastic little brother, and now it looks like you're a great detective, too.

Alex: Now let's get back to work on our project and see how impressive you are at making a thatched roof!

Reproducible 978-1-4129-5828-8 • © Corwin Press

Reader's Theater

A Day at the Beach
Cast of Characters: Ozwaldo, Danny, Jenna, Kyle, Hannah, Maria, Mr. Gazotti, Narrator

> **Scene One:** *Mr. Gazotti's class is on a field trip to the beach. They are working on a science unit on the environment. They have just gotten off the bus and walked to the shoreline.*

Mr. Gazotti: Okay kids, gather 'round.

Narrator: Mr. Gazotti's students congregate around their teacher near a tidepool on the shoreline.

Jenna: Wow, what a beautiful day! I haven't been to the beach in ages.

Hannah (pointing): Look out there! It's a dolphin!

Danny (smiling): Are you sure it's not a shark?

Hannah: Positive. The dorsal fins of a dolphin and of a shark look very different.

Ozwaldo: Besides, there are two other dolphins near the first, and they're swimming up and down. Sharks don't move like that.

Mr. Gazotti: Brilliant, Ozwaldo. That's true. What other varieties of animal life do you see?

Kyle: There are seals relaxing on that rock out there in the water.

Mr. Gazotti: Are you certain they are seals? Here, use these binoculars and examine them more carefully.

Narrator: Kyle studied the animals on the rock.

Kyle: Seals and sea lions resemble each other, but those animals are sea lions. I can tell because they have ear flaps. One of the sea lions has turned its tail fins under. Seals don't have ear flaps, and they don't do that with their fins.

Maria: I see plenty of seagulls. They are fishing over the ocean. There are other birds, too. See those white birds along the shoreline? They're called willets, and they have black and white stripes on their wings. They also have long beaks, and they are poking around in the wet sand.

Reader's Theater

A Day at the Beach (cont.)

Danny: What are they searching for?

Maria: They're searching for little crabs, snails, and worms that burrow down into the sand and mud.

Mr. Gazotti: Excellent!

Jenna: You don't need binoculars to see the creature I'm looking at. It's right here in the tidepool. It's a sea urchin. See all of its lavender spines? Those spines can grow back if they break off. Sea urchins eat kelp.

Mr. Gazotti: Can anyone explain to me what kelp is?

Danny: Kelp is seaweed . . . very big seaweed. It grows under water. Some animals live in kelp, and some animals eat it. Even people eat kelp.

Hannah: Look! There are sea stars in the pool. That one is a knobby star. It's a big one, too. They hold onto the rocks with lots of little tube feet. Even the waves can't wash them away. That one is probably looking for prey to eat.

Ozwaldo: It moves pretty slowly.

Hannah: That's okay. It eats snails that are even slower and barnacles that don't move at all.

Ozwaldo: There's another sea star. I know what that is. It's a brittle star, and it has thin arms that move very quickly.

Mr. Gazotti: I'm impressed that you've all been doing your homework. You even have a head start on the assignment you're going to complete while we're here. We're going to have a scavenger hunt.

Maria: Fabulous! I love scavenger hunts!

Narrator: Mr. Gazotti distributes paper and a pencil to each student.

Mr. Gazotti: On these sheets you'll find illustrations of five marine animals that are native to this beach. There is also a little information about each one. I'm going to assign you to groups of six. I want each group to try to find examples of these animals in their natural environment. You have already discovered the brittle star.

7

Reader's Theater

A Day at the Beach (cont.)

Danny: Do we have to capture the animal?

Mr. Gazotti: No, that wouldn't be right. Just circle the picture.

Narrator: Groups of students start walking along the shoreline.

Kyle: Look! There are a couple of brown pelicans, and they're on our list. It says they are the smallest of all the pelicans, but they look large to me.

Jenna: I wonder what the biggest pelicans look like.

Danny: We can circle the pelican on the paper and move on to the next animal. That means we only have three more animals to discover.

Ozwaldo: That's outstanding, because I'm getting hungry, and we have to finish this before we can eat lunch.

Hannah: Two of the other animals live in the tidepools. The other one lives in the sand. Let's look for the tidepool animals first.

Kyle: The animals in this illustration look cool. They're called hermit crabs. They live in abandoned shells. That shouldn't be too hard to spot.

Jenna: There are a bunch of crabs in this tidepool. There are a couple of different kinds, but I don't see any with shells.

Danny: That's a striped shore crab. Be careful, shore crabs can pinch, and they're fast, too. My dad and I go fishing down here sometimes. I've seen those crabs eat snails. They don't have to stay in the water, either; they do just fine on land.

Maria: We're looking for hermit crabs, and I don't see any in this tidepool. The other animal we need to find is an anemone. It looks more like a flower than an animal. According to this, it is a relative of the jellyfish.

Ozwaldo: There are plenty of anemones here. They have lots of soft tentacles, and you can see the tentacles moving in the water as the waves go by. Those things can sting. That's how they capture their food.

Kyle: Look at that! When that pebble rolled over it, the anemone disappeared. It curled up into the sand, so I guess that's how it protects itself from enemies.

7

Jenna: Would it sting if you touched it?

Reader's Theater

A Day at the Beach (cont.)

Ozwaldo: It says here that the stinging cells are too small to penetrate human skin, but I still don't think I'll try touching the anemone. When you're around tidepools, it's usually a good idea to just observe and keep your hands to yourself.

Danny: There are several barnacles on this rock. They look like part of the rock, but they are animals, too. They're attached to the rock, and they live inside those little cones. You want to be very careful around them. I stepped on some barnacles once when I was barefoot; those cones are razor sharp.

Hannah: We have two more animals to go.

Narrator: Maria calls to her friends from down the beach.

Maria: Come down here and see this tidepool! It's hermit crab central. There must be a dozen of them running around.

Jenna: They're adorable. Look, this one has a black shell. I recognize that. I believe it's called a black turban shell. Remember what Mr. Gazotti instructed before we came to the beach?

Hannah: Yes, he said not to take anything, even empty shells. I guess the reason is because an empty shell might eventually become a home for another animal.

Ozwaldo: Okay, we can circle the hermit crab. That leaves one more animal to discover, and we're going to have to dig for it. Sand crabs burrow down into the wet sand along the shoreline. That's what the shorebirds are looking for.

Danny: I know how to find them. Sometimes fishermen use the bigger ones as bait. First, you wait for a wave to wash up. When the wave goes out again, look for small bubbles in the sand and then dig immediately where the bubbles are located. The crabs can dig down fast, but if you're quick, you'll get a big handful of sand and a couple of sand crabs.

Narrator: The students wait for a wave to pass, and then they dig into the soggy, foamy sand.

Jenna: Awesome, I have one! It's still digging down, and it tickles!

Kyle: I think I have about three of them! Just brush the sand away, and you can see them. They're pretty miniscule. They don't have claws or spines, so they won't hurt you.

Maria: I guess that counts. We can circle the last animal and head back.

Ozwaldo: Fantastic! I'm absolutely starving.

Reader's Theater

The Surprise Guest
Cast of Characters: Isaiah, Benjamin, Brandon, Sophia, Ella, Nicole, Mrs. Romero, Mr. Dorfman

> ***Scene One:*** *Mrs. Romero's classroom. It is Monday, the first class of the day. Everyone is in their seats.*

Mrs. Romero: Good morning. I hope you all had a good weekend. I have a big surprise for you today.

Brandon: Homework has been cancelled for the week.

The class laughs.

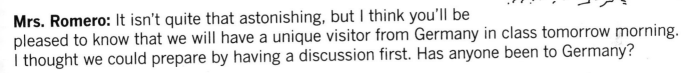

Mrs. Romero: It isn't quite that astonishing, but I think you'll be pleased to know that we will have a unique visitor from Germany in class tomorrow morning. I thought we could prepare by having a discussion first. Has anyone been to Germany?

Nicole: I went last year.

Mrs. Romero: That's wonderful, Nicole. Please tell us where you visited and a little something about it.

Nicole: I went to Munich with my grandparents, because that's where they're from. Munich is the third largest city in the country, so it's enormous and has a lot of people. We were there in the summer and it rained a lot, but it was very pretty. The city has lots of parks and museums. It isn't very far from the Alps, so people go skiing in the winter. After Munich, we traveled the Castle Road and saw some amazing castles.

Sophia: I've been to Germany, too. I was in the north in Hamburg. Hamburg is actually the second largest city. Berlin is the largest. Hamburg is a port city on the River Elbe, and there's a lot to do there. We went to a concert. Some famous composers were born there, like Brahms.

Isaiah: Why were you there?

Sophia: My dad travels a lot. He went there on business, so we got to go, too.

Mrs. Romero: Has anyone else traveled to Germany, or would anyone like to share anything they know about the country? Yes, Benjamin.

Benjamin: They have an excellent soccer league. The men's main professional league has eighteen teams. The women's league has twelve. The German women's team won the World Cup title in 2003. Only one team has a better record than they do.

8

Reader's Theater

The Surprise Guest (cont.)

Brandon: Really? What team is that?

Benjamin: The United States.

Ella: Awesome!

Mrs. Romero: I don't think our visitor plays soccer, but I understand that Sam mountain climbs, windsurfs, and snowboards. Does anyone know anything about these sports?

Ella: There is an indoor rock climbing center out by the interstate. I tried it a couple of times, and I like it a lot. You have to have a lot of strength in your arms and legs. There are lots of instructors there to help you learn.

Mrs. Romero: How is indoor climbing different from outdoor climbing?

Ella: The indoor climbing wall is man-made. The handholds and footholds are carved in or bolted on, so they can be changed. You don't have to worry about getting caught in a storm, either.

Benjamin: I saw a news story on television about a man who climbed up the side of a skyscraper. He climbed up eighty-eight stories and didn't use safety equipment or anything.

Ella: I don't think I'll be doing that anytime soon!

Nicole: It sounds like Sam is very adventurous when it comes to sports. When will he get here?

Mrs. Romero: The visit is scheduled for a few minutes after class begins. Can anyone tell us about windsurfing?

Isaiah: I've been windsurfing on the lake. It's a cross between surfing and sailing. The board has a sail on it that you hold on to and turn to catch the wind. I used a funboard, which is for beginners.

Brandon: I just read something in a magazine about indoor windsurfing. They do it in huge pools that are in giant tents.

Nicole: Are you serious?

Brandon: Yes, they use fans to create the wind. There was an indoor competition a while ago in London. I also read that they were building an indoor windsurfing pool in Germany.

Sophia: Maybe you can ask our guest about that.

Reader's Theater

The Surprise Guest (cont.)

Benjamin: Windsurfing and snowboarding are both Olympic sports. I watched snowboarding in the Winter Olympics a couple of years ago. There are special moves and maneuvers that the boarders have to do. It was exciting to watch!

Mrs. Romero: I don't think our guest will be turning up in the Olympics, but Sam is a great competitor. We'll learn all about that tomorrow. Now it's time to get to work.

> **Scene Two:** *Lunchtime. Benjamin, Brandon, Isaiah, Sophia, Ella, and Nicole are sitting at a table together.*

Sophia: The mystery guest for tomorrow sounds really cool.

Ella: I'll bet he's cute. I really like the fact that he plays all those sports. Maybe he has traveled all over Europe. Wouldn't that be great?

Brandon: You don't understand.

Nicole: What do you mean?

Brandon: Mrs. Romero never used the word *he*, even though we did. I think she's trying to surprise us. I think Sam is a girl.

Sophia: Really?

Isaiah: I think so, too. She said the visitor would be a big surprise.

Benjamin: She also said the visitor was unique.

Nicole: A girl that's good at sports isn't surprising or unique. Lots of girls are great at sports.

Ella: True, but now that you mention it, it did seem like there was something that Mrs. Romero wasn't saying.

Benjamin: Maybe the visitor is an older person. You know, someone who holds the snowboarding or windsurfing record for his or her age.

Sophia: Maybe it's just the opposite. Maybe the visitor really *is* a kid.

Brandon: Do you mean a very young kid? Like a kid in kindergarten?

Sophia: Yes. Maybe he or she is the youngest person ever to climb the world's tallest mountain, like Mount Everest.

Reader's Theater

The Surprise Guest (cont.)

Isaiah: If she's from Germany, maybe she climbed the tallest mountain in the Alps.

Brandon: I guess we'll have to wait until tomorrow to find out.

Scene Three: *Mrs. Romero's classroom. It is Tuesday morning, and everyone is waiting anxiously in their seats.*

Mrs. Romero: Good morning, class. Are you all enthusiastic about meeting our visitor?

Benjamin: Mrs. Romero, is our guest a boy or a girl?

Mrs. Romero: I don't want to spoil the surprise, but I suppose it's okay to tell you that our guest's name is Samantha, and she is a girl.

Brandon: I knew it!

Mrs. Romero: She's already here. Are you ready to meet her?

Benjamin: Definitely!

Enter Mr. Dorfman and a German shepherd.

Mrs. Romero: Class, please welcome Samantha and her trainer.

Isaiah: She's a German shepherd!

Mrs. Romero: That's right. Samantha is here to compete in the first ever Global Canine Athletic Competition. This is her trainer, Mr. Dorfman.

Mr. Dorfman: Hello, class. Thank you for inviting us to your school. I would like you to get to know Samantha. She is referred to as an avalanche dog. She works in the Alps to rescue people who have been trapped by falling snow and ice.

Brandon: That's amazing, but can she really windsurf and snowboard?

Mr. Dorfman: She can. I have to give her a little help, and we use specially designed boards. I have a film all about it. Would you like to see it?

Class (in unison): Absolutely!

Ella: She *is* cute!

Take It Home (Grades 4-6)

Form partnerships with parents as early as possible in the school year, so they can assist their child with repeated reading practice. Students can realize enormous growth in oral reading fluency when parents are enlisted as their partners in achieving this goal.

1. Invite parents to school for a repeated reading training session. Demonstrate for parents how to practice repeated reading and measure oral reading fluency.

2. Share research to illustrate the power of repeated reading. Use information from the "Put It Into Practice" section (page 8).

3. Contract with parents to listen to their child for 10 to 15 minutes, three to five times per week, as they practice repeated reading.

4. Make copies of the **Take It Home passages (pages 64–66)** for each student. Make sure parents record the time and sign the **Take It Home Accountability Form (below)** after each reading.

5. Ask parents to also read aloud challenging text to their child to stretch his or her receptive listening vocabulary.

Name: _____

Take It Home
Accountability Form

I want to become a fluent reader, so I have read my reading passage aloud at least three times. Please sign below if I read my passage to you three times.

Week of: _____

Monday: _____

Tuesday: _____

Wednesday: _____

Thursday: _____

Friday: _____

Week of: _____

Monday: _____

Tuesday: _____

Wednesday: _____

Thursday: _____

Friday: _____

Take It Home

A Wild Walk

Imagine that you are two hundred miles above the earth. You are traveling about ten times faster than a bullet. How would you like to step outside of your spacecraft and go for a walk? Astronauts do it all the time! It's called a spacewalk.

Astronauts perform a spacewalk to make repairs. They train for a long time to carry out a task. The first spacewalk took place in 1965. There have been a lot of spacewalks since then. To survive in space, an astronaut has to wear a special suit. The suit protects against harmful radiation. It controls the temperature. It regulates pressure and provides air to breathe.

Sometimes astronauts stay attached to the ship by a long tether. Usually they move freely. They use a rocket pack connected to the back of the spacesuit. The pack has tiny thrusters that release gas. These thrusters move the astronaut in the opposite direction.

No astronaut has been seriously harmed during a spacewalk. That doesn't mean it isn't dangerous. There is plenty of space junk orbiting Earth. The junk usually comes from old satellites. It also comes from earlier space missions. Remember that everything in orbit is moving very fast. Pieces as tiny as a grain of sand act like a bullet. A small hole in a spacesuit can be deadly. The suit can lose pressure.

At this time, the only person hit by space debris was a woman. She was hit in the shoulder by a small piece of fuel tank from a rocket. She was not injured. The woman was not on a spacewalk at the time. She was walking through a park in Tulsa, Oklahoma!

4

Name _____   Date _____

Take It Home

Boston Tea Party

   Can you picture a tea party that could lead to a war? The Boston Party did just that in 1773. It was a protest by American colonists against the British Tea Act. The protest was one event of several that led to the American Revolution.

   The colonists were angry that the British government was taxing them. The colonies were not represented in the government. They felt it was unfair to pay taxes they had no choice about. The problem grew when a British company was allowed to sell tea without paying the tax. Colonial merchants made a pact that they would not sell the tea. Ships loaded with tea entered Boston Harbor, but the cargo could not be unloaded. The captains of the ships wanted to leave. The governor wanted to obey the British law. He wanted the tea to be sold. He would not let the ships leave without delivering the cargo.

   There was a law that if the cargo was not delivered, it would be sold to pay the taxes due. That meant that the hated taxes would be paid one way or another. The colonists held meetings and decided to act. A group of about fifty colonists dressed up as Mohawk Indians. They crept aboard the ships. They cut open more than three hundred chests of tea and dumped the tea in the harbor. No other damage was done. Hundreds of Bostonians watched quietly. They were sending a message to the British.

   The British were very angry. They closed the port of Boston and passed laws to make life much harder in the colonies. Colonists in other cities protested and had tea parties of their own. Some even gave up tea and started drinking coffee. Before long, colonists became rebels. The thirteen colonies decided that the only solution was to fight for independence.

5

Take It Home

Magic Folk

People all over the world called fairies by different names. They were known as good folk, wee folk, or good neighbors. No matter what they were called, fairies came in many shapes and sizes. In Ireland, stories told of a magical race of tall, beautiful beings that came from far northern lands. According to legend, as the earth's magic seeped away, those fairies set sail for secret islands where it was always summer.

Fairies were divided into two types. Solitary fairies avoided humans and often other fairies. Brownies and leprechauns were solitary fairies. Trooping fairies traveled in groups. They included tiny winged creatures who wore glistening robes spun from spider silk. These little sprites loved music and often gathered in meadows under a starry sky to dance until dawn.

Fairies of both types could be good or bad. Many fairies did kind deeds for their human neighbors. They rewarded well-behaved people with good fortune. Brownies often lived near humans and were very helpful. The little creatures took care of farm animals. They did household chores and tended crops. They always worked secretly at night and vanished before dawn. In return, a wise farmer left out a bowl of sweet cream where the little fellows might find it.

Fairies had a dark side, too. When they wished, they drained the goodness from food and caused illness. Bruises and cramps resulted from pinches by invisible fairy hands. Anyone who ate the food of the fairies became hopelessly trapped in their magical world. There was one exception to the danger of fairy food—a certain cake given as a reward for kindness. The cake wasn't very tasty, but eating it brought luck and success to kind-hearted humans.

Keeping Track (Grades 4–8)

This method of repeated reading involves students keeping track of their own oral reading fluency scores over a period of time. When students assess and monitor their own fluency, motivation increases as they observe their growth.

1. Group students with partners according to their reading levels.

2. Select a set of ten appropriately leveled reading passages, such as the **Keeping Track passages (pages 69–73)** or other passages with cumulative word counts. A number of commercial programs have reading passages already marked, including Great Leaps (Campbell, 1996) at *www.greatleaps.com*, and Read Naturally (Ihnot, 2001) at *www.readnaturally.com*.

3. Place the reading passages inside plastic page protectors so students can mark the pages repeatedly. Each student will have his or her own set of passages.

4. Ask the first reader to read the first passage aloud for one minute (you will time and signal start and stop times) while his or her partner listens and circles errors by marking on the page protector using an erasable marker.

5. Partners work together to figure out the first reader's words correct per minute (words read minus errors) and mark the **Fluency Record Sheet reproducible (page 68)** accordingly.

6. The second reader reads the passage aloud for one minute (you will time and signal start and stop times) while his or her partner listens and circles any errors.

7. Partners then work together to figure out the second reader's words correct per minute and mark the form.

8. Students may practice reading their passages each day; however, at least one formal assessment should be recorded on the Fluency Record Sheet.

978-1-4129-5828-8

Name _____ Date _____

Fluency Record Sheet

Week of: _____

Day 1: _____ words read correctly

Day 2: _____ words read correctly

Day 3: _____ words read correctly

Day 4: _____ words read correctly

Week of: _____

Day 1: _____ words read correctly

Day 2: _____ words read correctly

Day 3: _____ words read correctly

Day 4: _____ words read correctly

Week of: _____

Day 1: _____ words read correctly

Day 2: _____ words read correctly

Day 3: _____ words read correctly

Day 4: _____ words read correctly

Week of: _____

Day 1: _____ words read correctly

Day 2: _____ words read correctly

Day 3: _____ words read correctly

Day 4: _____ words read correctly

Keeping Track

Weird Nests

    The Brazilian tree frog is a sculptor. It builds a nest of clay. The frog is an   (17)
amphibian, so it needs to lay its eggs near water. First, the male creates a   (32)
large shelf of clay. He then scoops a wide, saucer-shaped nest from the center.   (47)
The water-filled nest may be up to two feet across. When he is satisfied with the   (64)
work, the male calls out to let females know he has an excellent spot to lay eggs.   (81)
Once the eggs are in place, the parents leave. That is alright because the raised   (96)
nest keeps the eggs safe from fish that might eat them. It also protects the   (111)
tadpoles that hatch from the eggs.   (117)

    The nest of the African foam-nest tree frog is made mostly of air. After laying   (133)
her eggs, the female covers them with a thick mucus. The male and female beat   (148)
the mucus with their hind feet, whipping it into a foamy ball. The eggs become   (163)
suspended in the sticky mass. The parents then attach the ball to leaves   (176)
growing above the water. The eggs stay safe inside their nest, high above any   (190)
fish looking for a quick meal. When the eggs hatch, the tiny new tadpoles slip   (205)
into the water below.   (209)

Words Correct Per Minute: _____

4

Keeping Track

Is That for Real?

In 1912, the remains of tools were found in Piltdown, England. The skull and (14)
jawbone of a creature that may have used the tools were also dug from a gravel (30)
pit. The creature seemed to be half man and half ape. Scientists determined (43)
that the "ancient" fossils were more than one million years old. They named the (57)
find the Piltdown Man. Not long after, they decided that it was actually a woman. (72)
Over time, researchers announced more findings. They said the creature had (83)
been a vegetarian, and it had not been able to speak when it was alive. (98)

It would not be until 1953 that the true facts came to be known. The Piltdown (114)
Man was a clever fake! The skull belonged to a modern human. The jawbone (128)
was that of an orangutan with teeth from another animal. The bones had been (142)
stained to look older. To their credit, some people had already suggested (154)
that the fossils were a fake. The new mystery was who was responsible for (168)
the incredible hoax? Some people blamed the scientists who had made the (180)
discovery. Some thought the workmen who found the remains were behind (191)
the joke. Others believed that the author of Sherlock Holmes had planted the (204)
"fossils" as a prank. What do *you* think? (212)

Words Correct Per Minute: _____

5

Keeping Track

The Lost Dutchman's Mine

    Over two centuries ago, the king of Spain granted land in Arizona to a local family. (16)
Apache Indians killed those who came to claim it. A survivor drew a map that he (32)
declared led to a rich mine. (38)

    In 1870, another man came and befriended his Apache neighbors. They led him to (52)
a canyon where he saw nuggets of gold. They let him take what he could carry, which (69)
turned out to be worth over six thousand dollars. When he tried to return to the mine, (86)
he was killed. (89)

    Later, two German prospectors purchased the rights to the land from the owners. (102)
At first they worked peacefully, and records show that they brought out nuggets (115)
worth thousands of dollars. When one of the miners was killed under mysterious (128)
circumstances, his partner fled for his life without revealing the location of the gold. (142)
The Apaches filled in the mine and toppled rock landmarks. Only one landmark (155)
remained, a sharp pinnacle of rock. Mistaking the German accents of the miners (168)
for Dutch, the locals called the place the Lost Dutchman's Mine, and most people (182)
believed it was cursed. (186)

    Later, two soldiers rode into a town with their saddlebags filled with gold nuggets. (200)
They mentioned a landmark, a pinnacle of rock, before riding out to gather more (214)
treasure. When the soldiers failed to return, a search party discovered their bodies. (227)

    The last known victim of the mine's curse set out in 1931. He said he had the (244)
original map. His headless body was recovered a short time later. Does wealth still (258)
wait in the mountains, or does something else wait for those unlucky enough to find it? (274)

Words Correct Per Minute: _____

Keeping Track

The Minotaur

Greek myth is filled with stories of unusual creatures. One is the tale of the (15)
Minotaur. The story supposedly began with Minos, a powerful king of the island of (29)
Crete. He was so powerful that he risked angering the gods by refusing to sacrifice a (45)
beautiful white bull in their honor. This made the gods angry, so to punish Minos, they (61)
saw to it that his next child was born with the head of a bull. Called the Minotaur, the (80)
creature was so awful that Minos had to hide it away in a twisting maze deep beneath (97)
his palace. Over many years, the Minotaur grew big and strong, but it had the mind of (114)
a vicious beast. When it was hungry for the human flesh it preferred to eat, its terrible (131)
roars echoed through the halls above. (137)

Meanwhile, the warriors of Crete had beaten the soldiers of Athens in battle. The (151)
defeated city of Athens was forced to send a yearly tribute to Crete of seven young (167)
Athenian boys and girls doomed to enter the Minotaur's maze. It was not the sort (182)
of thing anyone would volunteer for, but one young man did just that. He was the (198)
handsome son of the Athenian king. When he arrived on Crete, Minos's daughter (211)
fell in love with him. Before he entered the maze, she gave him a small sharp sword (228)
and a ball of twine. He tied one end of the twine to the maze door and unraveled the (247)
ball behind him as he searched for the Minotaur. With the sword and the element of (263)
surprise in his favor, the Athenian managed to kill the monster and escaped the maze (278)
by following the twine to safety. (284)

Words Correct Per Minute: _____

7

Keeping Track

A Changing Land

The land surface of the earth has not always looked as it does today. In fact, the (17) continents are constantly moving very slowly. In a process that takes many millions of (31) years, they pull apart and merge together over and over. Almost three hundred million (45) years ago, the land on Earth's surface was made up of a single supercontinent. Over (60) time, geological forces split the giant continent into the multiple continents we know (73) today. The Great Rift Valley of East Africa is one of the few places on dry land where (91) people can observe these geological forces at work. (99)

About twenty million years ago, in what is now East Africa, magma thrust its way (114) upward. The land above the magma lifted and commenced to split and crack, creating (128) a fissure that would extend over two thousand miles. As the rift opened, it fashioned (143) fantastic valleys bordered by towering cliffs. In some places, the cliffs soar two (156) thousand feet straight up from the valley floor. (164)

A triangle of land at the northern end of the rift is actually an enormous section of (181) sea floor. This region was once at the bottom of a nearby sea. But as the land rose, the (200) salt water became shallow and eventually evaporated. It left behind a layer of salt that (215) is three miles thick in some places. (222)

The rift splits into two branches that join again near the southern end of the valley (238) where the world's second deepest lake fills a deep, wide opening in the western (252) branch. Two of the world's largest volcanoes tower over the eastern branch. Lake (265) Victoria, the source of the Nile River, is between the two branches. (277)

Words Correct Per Minute: _____

CHAPTER 6

Phrased Reading

Encourage Fluency Through Phrased Reading

Besides being able to decode automatically, fluent readers chunk or parse text into syntactically appropriate units, mainly phrases (Rasinski, 2003). A dysfluent reader has great difficulty parsing or chunking text so that it makes sense. Practicing reading in phrases helps students learn to break text into meaningful parts. Phrased reading should take place several times per week for about ten minutes per day.

1. Provide students with copies of the **Phrased Reading passages (pages 75–84)**, utilizing the appropriate reading level.

2. Read aloud the segmented passage with appropriate phrasing and intonation. Ask students if they can figure out what the markers indicate. Then discuss why phrasing is important in the fluent reading process.
   a. The single slash indicates a slight pause.
   b. The double slash after the period indicates a more prolonged pause.

3. As a class, rehearse a passage in unison. Remind students that the phrase markers identify chunks of text that should be smoothly read together.

4. Provide students with time to read segmented passages with partners.

5. Allow students to rehearse segmented passages independently.

6. Meet with students individually to hear independent readings of segmented passages. Note students' expression, pauses, and phrasing. Assist those who seem to struggle.

7. Provide students with an unsegmented passage. If using the Phrased Reading passages provided, you may choose to white out the slash marks.

Phrased Reading

Digging for Fossils

Fossils are the remains of animals or plants/ that lived long ago.// Some may be/ as much as 600 million years old!// A fossil is any trace/ of a living thing.// That might include/ footprints, droppings, burrows, leaf impressions,/ or root tunnels.// It can include/ shells, eggshells, skin impressions,/ or bones.// Not all living things become fossils.// Most of the animals/ that lived millions of years ago/ are gone forever.// Animal parts that became fossils/ were usually hard.// Shells, teeth, and bones/ are the most common.// Conditions had to be just right for softer material,/ like skin,/ to remain.// Sometimes insects were trapped/ in sticky tree sap.// The sap hardened.// The tiny insect was preserved.// In dry places,/ an animal could become a mummy.// If the animal was buried quickly,/ its skin could dry out.// Mummies are rare.//

A fossil may have formed/ when an animal died in water.// The animal may have drowned.// A flood may have washed/ its body out to sea.// Slowly, sand or mud/ covered the remains.// Over time,/ more layers of mud covered the body/ until it was deeply buried.// The flesh rotted away,/ but the bones and teeth remained.// Minerals in the water/ seeped into the bones.// The minerals replaced/ the remains with rock.//

Probably/ thousands of fossils are still buried.// They cannot be discovered/ until they are exposed.// For example,/ over millions of years/ an old seabed might be forced upward.// Slowly,/ wind and rain wear away the rock.// At last/ the fossil is exposed.// Sometimes/ workers find a fossil/ when they dig out a site/ for a new building.//

Once found,/ a fossil has to be handled carefully.// First,/ scientists make a drawing/ or map of the site.// They may take photographs/ of the fossil in place.// Good records offer clues/ about the fossil/ when it is studied in the laboratory.// When scientists are ready to dig,/ they spray the exposed parts of the fossil/ with a special glue.// This hardens the parts/ that may have cracked or weakened.// Then,/ they dig with larger tools,/ such as hammers and chisels.// They use small scrapers and brushes/ close to the bone.// Often,/ they dig up the fossil/ with plenty of rock around it.// The scientists mix up a big batch of plaster.// They cover the fossil and rock/ with plaster and strips of strong fabric.// Once the covering is dry,/ a scientist labels the fossil/ with a date and location.// Each fossil is carefully placed in a crate/ with lots of padding.// In the laboratory,/ other scientists prepare the fossils to be studied.//

Phrased Reading

Digging for Fossils (cont.)

Would you like to search for fossils?// You can find them in many places/ if you know what to look for.// The best place to look/ is in sedimentary rock.// This is a kind of rock/ that formed when layers of sand, silt, or mud/ hardened into rock.// Sometimes/ parts of plants or animals/ were buried within the layers.// The parts were preserved/ as the rock hardened.//

Begin your fossil hunt/ with a little research.// Read about/ the geography of your area.// Talk to geologists at local schools.// You might find a rock hound club/ in your area.// They can tell you/ about the best places to search.// Start where you can find/ lots of exposed rock.// Rocky beaches, riverbanks,/ or at the base of low cliffs are all good places to look.// You can also try your luck/ in areas that have been cleared/ for construction or highways.//

There are plenty of rules/ that you need to know.// Many local, state, and federal park laws/ don't permit you to take specimens.// If the land is privately owned,/ get permission to explore.// If you get permission,/ be sure to leave everything/ the way you found it.// Cover holes,/ close gates,/ and take your trash with you.// Never go out alone/ and be sure that someone at home knows/ where you will be.// Learn about any dangers,/ such as snakes or slide areas.// Always bring a map,/ a compass,/ and plenty of water.//

You'll need a few tools.// Your kit should have a small rock hammer,/ a scraper, brushes, plastic bags, gloves, safety glasses,/ and a notebook.// Keep records of what you find/ and where you found it.// Once you bring your samples home,/ clean them carefully.// Label each one/ with a date and place.// Keep your treasures safe/ in a sample box.// You can also display them.// If you find something that is very interesting,/ take it to a local geology group.// It might be an important discovery!//

 978-1-4129-5828-8 • © Corwin Press

Phrased Reading

The Treasure

   "Six days,"// Jason moaned aloud.// "I'm stuck here/ for six whole days!"// He flopped down on the end of the bed/ and glanced around the room.// The wallpaper was a mass of delicate pink flowers,/ and lacy curtains hung at the windows.// Jason enjoyed sleeping late during vacation,/ but he knew that on his uncle's farm/ everyone was up at daybreak.//

   "So, what do you think?"/ a voice behind him asked.// Jason turned to see/ his cousin, Andrew.// Jason and Andrew got along well.// They had a lot of things in common.// They were both excellent skateboarders,/ and they both loved to read mysteries.//

   "It's okay,"/ Jason fibbed.//

   Andrew grinned.// "No, it isn't.// This was Great Grandma Hattie's bedroom/ when she was a little girl.// I don't think it's changed a bit/ since she lived here.// Dad likes to keep it this way/ because it reminds him of her.// Come on,/ my room's a lot better."// Andrew was correct.// The walls in his bedroom/ were plastered with colorful posters/ of skateboarders and basketball players.//

   "This one's really good,"/ Andrew said,/ handing his cousin a paperback book.// "It's about a kid/ who finds treasure/ in an abandoned mine."//

   Jason took the book.// "That would be so cool."// He sat cross-legged on the floor/ and glanced through the illustrations.// "I wish/ we could search for treasure.// You don't have any condemned mines close by,/ do you?"//

   Andrew raised one eyebrow.// "Do you know/ that Jesse James used to live around here?// People say/ some of his treasure has never been found.// There's a dried-up well/ about a mile from here.// It looks like a perfect place/ to hide something."//

   "Do you think it was here back then?"/ Jason asked excitedly.//

   "I don't know for sure,/ but we could go check it out anyway," Andrew said.//

   The boys filled a backpack with a garden spade,/ a flashlight, gloves, and sandwiches.// The well was near a stand of gnarly pine trees/ that offered shade while they explored.//

   "There's a board over the top,"/ Andrew explained/ as they stood looking at a low ring of rocks.// It created a ledge/ that marked the position of the well.//

Phrased Reading

The Treasure (cont.)

Jason helped his cousin lift the faded board,/ and then he knelt and peered underneath/ with a flashlight.// A surprised lizard scurried out/ and dashed under a bush.//

"Let's try digging around,"/ Jason suggested.// As he stepped forward,/ the old board teetered/ and tipped over,/ causing a jagged rock to tumble.// It rolled to one side/ as a shower of pebbles followed.// "Look!"/ Andrew exclaimed.// "What's that?"//

The corner of a metal box/ glimmered from an opening/ in the rock wall.// Using the spade,/ Andrew pried a couple more rocks away,/ and Jason tugged the box/ from its hiding place.//

"It's locked,"/ he announced while shaking the box.// "It sounds like there's something in here,/ but it isn't heavy."//

"My dad will open it,"/ Andrew said.// "He's going to be surprised."//

A short time later,/ Andrew and Jason stood in the kitchen/ watching with anticipation/ as Andrew's dad pried at the lock/ with a miniature screwdriver.// Andrew's mom sat next to him.// "I don't know where it came from,"/ she said kindly.// "But it doesn't look old enough/ to have belonged to Jesse James."//

"I think I've got it,"/ Andrew's dad said/ as the lock clicked.// Slowly/ he opened the lid,/ and everyone looked inside.// A small doll/ with curly brown hair/ and glass eyes/ gazed up at them.// Beside her was a note/ and a little gold locket.//

"What does the note say,/ Uncle Ben?"/ Jason asked.//

The older man's eyes grew misty/ as he read the fine writing.// "It's a letter/ from my Grandmother Hattie.// This was her favorite doll.// She concealed it here/ to keep it safe from a storm.// I imagine that must have been/ when her parents died/ and she went to live in St. Louis/ with her aunt.// By the time she was old enough to come back,/ she had probably forgotten about it."// He opened the tiny locket.// In it were pictures/ of a lovely woman/ and a handsome young man.// "These are your great-great grandparents,"/ he said/ as he held out the locket/ for Andrew to see.//

Jason smiled/ as he gazed at the miniature photographs.// "I guess we really did find a treasure after all."//

Phrased Reading

The History of Candy

The word *candy* comes from an Arab word/ for a lump of sugar cane.// Honey from bees/ was the first sweet treat/ enjoyed by ancient humans.// Egyptians were likely to have created the first candies/ from dried fruits, nuts, and even flowers/ drizzled with honey.// It was sticky but tasty.// Scientists have uncovered evidence/ that Middle Eastern, Chinese, Greek, and Roman cultures/ ate candy treats made from similar ingredients.// India first introduced sugar cane.// It is a giant grass/ harvested from river deltas.// At first,/ people just enjoyed/ chewing the sweet cane.// Later,/ many cultures made syrup from the plant.//

Europeans of the Middle Ages/ were aware of candy,/ but the cost of sugar was too high.// Only the very wealthy/ could afford to eat it.// When explorers returned from the New World/ in the early sixteenth century,/ they brought chocolate.// Once again,/ only the wealthy/ could enjoy the dark treasure.// European candies/ also included some spices.// People believed/ that the small treats aided digestion.//

Easier access to ingredients/ and a drop in the price of sugar/ made chocolate and other candy more affordable/ in the seventeenth century.// In the American colonies,/ hard candies were all the rage.// Colonists enjoyed/ peppermints and lemon drops.// In what would one day be New York City,/ candy makers created marzipan/ from ground almonds.// Molasses and maple syrup/ were also popular sweeteners.// The use of sugar beet juice/ allowed mass production of "penny candy,"/ which were made available to children.//

A turning point occurred/ when Swiss candy makers introduced milk chocolate/ in 1875.// Today,/ chocolate bars may be filled with a wide array of sweets,/ such as sugar, chocolate, caramel, fruit, nuts, marshmallows, coffee beans, peanut butter,/ and even alcohol.//

Phrased Reading

The History of Candy (cont.)

Among candy favorites in America/ is Cracker Jack®.// Frederick William Rueckheim invented Cracker Jack.// When he came to Chicago in the late 1800s,/ he sold popcorn from a cart.// With his brother,/ he developed a popcorn and peanut treat/ covered in molasses.// They introduced it at the Chicago World's Fair/ in 1893.// The Ferris wheel, Aunt Jemima® pancakes, and the ice-cream cone/ were presented at the same fair.// The company added the well-known "surprise" in every package/ in 1912.//

Some candies/ are eaten on particular holidays.// Peeps® are a marshmallow candy/ sold to celebrate Easter, Halloween, and Christmas.// The Egyptians first made sweet marshmallow/ from the sap of the marshmallow plant.// In the 1800s,/ doctors used the plant juice to make a candy/ that soothed coughs.// Later,/ plant sap was replaced with gelatin in the recipe.// Peeps, shaped like bright yellow chicks,/ were introduced in about 1940.// Now the sweet treat/ is sold in many shapes, colors, and sizes.//

Another holiday treat,/ the candy cane,/ has been around for over three hundred years!// This favorite was born/ when a German choir master bent sugar sticks/ into a cane shape.// He handed them out to children/ to keep them quiet during church services.// The first canes were white.// Striped, peppermint-flavored canes/ showed up much later.//

A very popular brand of candy of the modern age/ is M&Ms® Plain Chocolate Candy.// M&Ms were developed by Forrest Mars Sr.// On a trip to Spain,/ he saw soldiers eating chocolate drops/ in a hard sugar coating.// He recognized a good idea,/ and his version of the candy/ was first sold in 1941.// United States soldiers carried the treats/ as snacks.// M&Ms® Peanut Chocolate Candies/ went on sale in 1954.// The plain chocolate candies/ were the first candies/ to ride into space on the shuttle.// As part of the astronaut food supply,/ they are on display at the National Air and Space Museum in Washington, DC.//

978-1-4129-5828-8 • © Corwin Press

Phrased Reading

The History of Cell Phones

A cell phone is/ a wireless telephone.// The cell phone user can make a call/ from home, school, the office,/ and even while riding in a car.// A cell phone system uses base stations/ to create service areas, or cells.// Calls shift from base station to base station/ as the caller travels/ from one cell to another.//

To understand the history of the cell phone,/ you have to begin in the nineteenth century.// Back then,/ scientist Michael Faraday/ was studying electromagnetism.// He wondered if electromagnetic waves/ could be sent through the air.// At the same time,/ scientist James Maxwell/ predicted the existence of radio waves.// Their work set the stage/ for the development of such things/ as radio, television, and cell phones.// In 1865,/ a New York dentist named Mahlon Loomis/ applied for a patent.// He claimed to be the first person/ to send a wireless signal/ through the atmosphere.// Although no one was there to confirm it,/ Loomis declared that he used kites as antennae.// He then sent a signal/ from one mountaintop to another/ in Virginia.// A little more than twenty years later,/ witnesses watched as Giglielmo Marconi/ sent and received the first radio signal.//

By the 1920s,/ radios were widely used.// The car radio was developed/ shortly after.// It became an important tool/ for police officers and taxicabs.// A decade later,/ a portable two-way radio was designed/ for the United States military.// Bell Laboratories presented/ the idea of cellular communications/ in 1947.// It was a great concept/ for people who needed to stay in touch/ while they were on the move.// At first/ the phones were used/ only in vehicles.// Later designs included a cigarette lighter plug/ so the phone could be removed/ and carried around.// The Bell Laboratory scientists suggested/ that by creating small areas,/ or cells, of service/ with special towers,/ the phones would be more mobile.// But the technology didn't exist/ at the time.//

Phrased Reading

The History of Cell Phones (cont.)

The Federal Communications Commission (FCC) regulated all broadcasts.// As the number of mobile phone users grew,/ they needed more frequencies/ to carry messages.// The FCC limited the frequencies/ to twenty-three.// That meant only a few calls/ could be made at any one time.// That led to interference/ and long waits for a free line.// With such a small market,/ companies weren't rushing/ to develop the technology needed.// By 1968,/ the FCC changed course/ and assigned additional frequencies.// The Bell Laboratory idea/ of setting up cells/ was now possible.// A network of cell sites could "hand off" calls/ from tower to tower as the caller moved/ from one location to another.//

Martin Cooper began to work/ for the Motorola Company/ in 1954.// He started by working/ on handheld police radio systems.// Within two decades,/ he and his coworkers were developing/ the first wireless portable phone.// The two-pound prototype was called a shoe phone/ because it looked a little like a boot.// The engineers had to come up/ with tiny parts to fit in the small space.// In April of 1973,/ Cooper became the first person to make a call/ on a cell phone.// Once the phone was ready,/ engineers had to design a system/ that would enable their portable phone to operate.// Low-power transmitters had to overlap/ to prevent dropped calls.// Computers had to track callers/ as they moved through the system.// The systems were tested/ in Chicago, New York, and Washington, DC.// Shortly afterward,/ the FCC approved the system,/ and cell phones were made available/ to the general public in 1984.// They were bulky, hard to carry,/ and cost several thousand dollars.// Within three years,/ more than a million people had cell phones.//

Today, digital cell phones are so small/ users can carry them in a shirt pocket.// They are also fairly inexpensive/ and have lots of features.// They come in a variety of colors/ and covers that slip, slide, and twist.// Some people depend only on a cell phone/ and do not own a landline phone.// Even young children carry cell phones/ in their backpacks.// Cell phones can be used/ to take photographs, text-message, watch videos, play games,/ send emails,/ and even access the Internet.// Michael Faraday would be amazed!

7

Phrased Reading

The History of the Internet

In 1945,/ Vannevar Bush wrote an article/ for the *Atlantic Monthly* magazine.// In it he described/ a future that included a workspace/ with a keyboard and glowing screen.// He envisioned a machine/ that was a file and a library/ that could be accessed from anywhere.//

Bush was the Director/ of the Office of Scientific Research and Development/ of the United States.// He organized a research partnership/ between the military and universities.// Funding from the partnership/ later helped MIT to create the famed Lincoln Laboratory.// The people in this partnership/ wanted computers to share information/ on research and development/ in scientific and military fields.// They planted the seed of the Internet.//

Research heated up/ when the Soviet Union launched the first artificial earth satellite,/ *Sputnik I*, in 1957.// Worried that the USSR would take the lead in science and technology,/ the United States created the Advanced Research Projects Agency, or ARPA.// The agency operated/ as part of the Department of Defense.// The concept was to provide a communications network/ that would keep working,/ even if a nuclear attack destroyed some of its sites.//

ARPA selected J. C. R. Licklider of MIT/ to head their Information Processing Techniques Office.// He had already been promoting the idea/ of a global network of computers/ that allowed users to access data/ from anywhere in the world.// In 1963,/ Larry Roberts of Lincoln Laboratory/ and others joined his group.// Licklider made agreements/ with MIT, the University of California at Los Angeles (UCLA), and the research firm BBN/ to start work on his plan.//

In 1965,/ Larry Roberts was ready to conduct a test.// He connected a computer in Massachusetts/ with a computer in California.// He did it over dial-up telephone lines.// From this,/ researchers learned/ that telephone lines could work,/ but they were inefficient and expensive.// The scientists decided/ to use a new idea called packet switching/ to send information.// First,/ the information/ was broken into small units.// Next,/ it was labeled/ with where it came from/ and where it was going.// The information could then/ be passed from computer to computer.//

Within two years/ ARPA researchers met/ at a conference in Michigan.// Roberts explained his plan/ for the ARPANET.// They decided that a special computer/ called an Interface Message Processor, or IMP,/ should connect the network.// It worked like the routers of today.// Researchers first sent information/ between UCLA,/ Stanford Research Institute,/ University of California at Santa Barbara,/ and University of Utah in 1969.//

Phrased Reading

The History of the Internet (cont.)

In those days/ there were no personal computers/ in homes or offices.// Then Intel released the first microprocessor chip.// Computers could be smaller, cheaper, and faster.// The concept of email soon followed,/ and the symbol @ was chosen to link usernames and addresses.// Scientists Vinton Cerf and Bob Khan developed a new protocol called TCP/IP.// The changes made working with the computers easier.// In 1977,/ Steve Wozniak and Steve Jobs announced the Apple II computer.// At last, computers were available and affordable/ for the public.// As the commands became standardized,/ it was simpler for people to learn to use the nets/ that were being developed.//

By 1982,/ the computer was honored on a *Time* magazine cover/ as its "Man of the Year!"// The ARPANET was retired/ and transferred to the National Science Foundation system in 1990.// Before long,/ universities and research facilities in Europe and the United States were linked.// The government of the United States soon turned management/ over to independent online services such as Delphi, AOL, and Prodigy.// Although portable computers were still a thing of the future,/ desktop units were common in offices and even homes.// The University of Wisconsin produced a Domain Name System/ that made it easier to access other servers.//

Today, Internet users enjoy/ Web pages, chat rooms, message boards, and online sales.// The trend is toward high-speed and wireless connections/ and Internet access through smart phones and pocket PCs.// The dream of scientists has become a reality/ and an important part of global culture.//

CHAPTER 7

Assessing Fluency

How to Measure Reading Fluency

Oral reading fluency is measured by asking a student to read an appropriate passage of about 150–250 words, depending on the grade level. Readability estimates can be determined using various readability formulas and classroom materials. If you use your own passages, select those with minimal dialogue and few unusual names or words.

Photocopy the **Assessing Fluency passages (pages 86–95)**. Select an appropriate passage for the student's grade level. Time the student as he or she reads. After one minute, mark the last word read. Count the words read. Generally, omissions, insertions, and self-corrections are not counted as errors. Substitutions and incorrectly identified words are counted as errors. The score that counts is the number of words read correctly in one minute. Subtract the number of errors from the total number of words read to determine words correct per minute.

Acceptable Levels of Reading Fluency

Oral reading fluency is a combination of accuracy and rate. The fluency score is reported as words correct per minute. The minimum acceptable target oral reading fluency rates vary by grade level and text difficulty.

Grade	Fall	Winter	Spring
1	--	52	60
2	53	73	82
3	79	107	115
4	99	115	118
5	105	129	134
6	115	132	140
7	140	140	140
8	140	140	140

Source: Adapted from Marston and Magnusson (1988) and Rasinski (2003).

Reading fluency rates are an excellent indicator of reading proficiency. However, once students have reached an oral reading fluency rate of 140 words correct per minute, the question of rate is moot. When students can read rapidly and accurately, they focus on expression, voice projection, and clarity of speech.

Assessing Fluency

A Sticky Pastime

Blowing bubbles with bubble gum can be a fun hobby. At least it is for the   (16)
world's champion bubble blowers. One annual contest draws nearly a million   (27)
entries across the country. The six finalists gather to see who can blow the   (41)
largest bubble within five minutes. All of the contestants receive savings bonds, (53)
and the winner gets a whopping ten thousand dollars! One winner blew a bubble   (67)
seventeen inches wide. The world record bubble was a huge twenty-three   (79)
inches across!   (81)

Experts say the largest bubbles come from gum that contains sugar. Such   (93)
gum is usually hard and sticky. It needs a lot of chewing. Some people like to   (109)
chew more than one piece of gum at a time. To compete for the world record,   (125)
you can have no more than three pieces of gum in your mouth. It is safer to   (142)
work indoors to avoid wind that might pop the bubble. Air temperature is   (155)
important, too. If the bubble is brittle, the air is too cold. If it sags, the air is (173)
too warm. Chew the gum to make it soft. Form as large a wad as possible in   (190)
the front of your mouth. Use your tongue to create a pocket. Keep your lips   (205)
loose as you slowly blow air into the bubble. Good luck!   (216)

Words Correct Per Minute: _____

Assessing Fluency

The Southern Continent

What do you think of when you picture a desert? Do you see sand and rocks? (16)
Do you imagine hot temperatures? Believe it or not, a desert can be covered (30)
with snow and ice. A desert is any place that receives less than ten inches of (46)
new moisture per year. The new moisture can be in the form of rain or snow. (62)
Antarctica has an average of less than four inches of new snow per year. That (77)
makes Antarctica a cold desert. (82)

Antarctica is the most southern of Earth's continents. It is also the coldest (95)
place on the planet. Temperatures can drop below minus one hundred degrees. (107)
Still, not all of the continent is completely covered with ice and snow. There are (122)
a few dry valleys of frozen sand and rock. Some of those valleys even have small (138)
streams. They form from melted water under nearby glaciers. There are even (150)
a few small lakes. Minerals in the water prevent the lakes from freezing solid. (164)
Icecaps at the surface keep lake water fairly warm. The bottom temperature of (177)
one lake was measured at times at almost eighty degrees. (187)

Penguins and seals live along the shorelines of Antarctica. Some insects have (199)
been discovered. A wingless fly, less than a quarter-inch long, is considered the (213)
largest land animal living on the continent! (220)

Words Correct Per Minute: _____

Late
4

Assessing Fluency

Dragons

According to legends, dragons formed when time itself began. When there (11)
was no order yet in the world, these horrible beasts roamed at will. The scaly (26)
dragons of Europe were a cruel bunch. Some lived in swamps, their steamy (39)
breath rising above the murky water. Some dragons lived in dark caves. The (52)
bones of their victims surrounded them. Dragons came in dozens of shapes (64)
and sizes. Some were two feet long. Others were one hundred times that. Many (78)
were wormlike with poisonous breath that could choke a human in seconds. (90)
They used their sharp teeth to grasp prey but usually swallowed their prey in (104)
one piece. (106)

The savage western dragon had four legs tipped with razor-sharp claws. Its (119)
tail carried a deadly sting, and its poisonous sweat could shrivel plants. Smoke (132)
and fire streamed from its nostrils. A dragon could be green, brown, red, or (146)
black, but it always had gleaming red eyes. This monster had excellent vision. (159)
With leathery wings, it flew over the countryside searching for victims. It usually (172)
ate cattle and an occasional human, particularly tender young princesses. (182)
Oddly, this dragon also loved milk and cream. In exchange for a large barrel of (197)
milk every day, the dragon could be persuaded to leave a village unharmed. (210)

Words Correct Per Minute: _____

Early 5

Assessing Fluency

Seeing Is Believing . . . or Not

    Can you always believe what you see? Not really. A mirage is a trick of the (16)
light that creates the illusion of water. On a hot day you might see a pool of (33)
water on the road ahead only to watch it disappear as you get closer. The image (49)
is really a reflection of the blue sky above. In a hot desert during the day, the (66)
air layer nearest the ground is often warmer than the air layer above. Light (80)
rays bend toward the cooler layer of air, so the light is directed up toward your (96)
eyes. You might also see reflections of distant objects. Your eye receives both (109)
the direct rays of light from the object and light rays that bounce up from the (125)
ground. So if you are seeing a tree, you see the real tree and an upside-down (142)
tree below it. (145)

    Mirages also appear at sea. The phenomena are called *Fata Morgana*. In calm (158)
weather, warm air over cold water produces an upside-down image. The image (171)
appears to hover over the water. Travelers report seeing boats and icebergs (183)
drifting through the sky in Arctic waters. This is called looming. In 1906, Arctic (197)
explorer Robert Peary drew a mysterious island on his maps. He called it (210)
Crockerland. It turned out to have been a mirage. (219)

Words Correct Per Minute: _____

Assessing Fluency

The Kola Nut

What do certain trees in Africa and a bottle of cola have in common? It's the kola   (17)
nut. It grows on a tall tree with long leaves and star-shaped fruit. The nut is used as a   (37)
flavoring in some popular cola drinks.   (43)

The kola nut has been used in Africa for hundreds of years. Arab traders often   (58)
carried the nuts on long journeys. Travelers claimed that chewing on the nuts gave   (72)
them energy and strength and also kept them from getting hungry and thirsty. In fact,   (87)
the earliest cola drinks were sold as a type of medicine rather than a treat.   (102)

In ancient times, the price of kola nuts was often high, so they were considered a   (118)
luxury in African cultures. Even today, visitors may be welcomed to a home with an   (133)
offering of kola nuts. They are also served at special occasions, such as weddings, and   (148)
sometimes are included in a bride's dowry.   (155)

The nuts may be eaten whole, but it takes a while to get used to the taste. Kola nuts   (174)
are bitter at first, and then the taste becomes sweet. Some fans of the kola nut prefer   (191)
to dry it and grind it into a powder, which can be mixed with water to make a sweet   (210)
drink. When a toothbrush isn't handy, twigs from the tree are even used to clean the   (226)
teeth and gums.   (229)

Words Correct Per Minute: _____

Assessing Fluency

A Summer Treat

    The frozen ice pop has been around for centuries. During Roman times, runners (13)
brought blocks of ice from the mountains. The ice was crushed and mixed with fruit (28)
and syrup. Other cultures did the same, using fruit pulp, fruit syrup, and flowers (42)
for flavor. (44)

    In the nineteenth century, street vendors in cities sold penny ices that were like (58)
snow cones. At the beginning of the twentieth century, an eleven-year-old boy mixed (73)
up some soda water, powder, and water. It was a popular drink in those days. He left (90)
the concoction on the porch with the stick in the cup. That night, temperatures in (105)
California reached record lows. When the boy woke the next morning, he found that (119)
he had a tasty ice treat on a stick. The following summer, he made ice pops in his (137)
family's icebox and sold them to his neighbors and friends. In 1922, he introduced (151)
the ice lollipop to the general public and received a patent the following year. The (166)
treat was eventually called the Popsicle® and made available in seven flavors. (178)

    The twin-pop came along during the Depression so kids could share the treat. (192)
The sticks used to hold the treat are also very popular. First made from birchwood, (207)
today they are made of basswood. In one year, more than a billion sticks may be (223)
manufactured. That's enough to circle the earth many times. Sticks are a popular (236)
craft item, as kids everywhere turn them into homemade fans or picture frames. (249)

Words Correct Per Minute: _____

Assessing Fluency

Firewalkers

In Fiji, a rite is performed that takes intense mental preparation. A priest leads the (15)
faithful on a barefoot stroll over a pit of fiery stones. The pit is about four feet deep (33)
and twenty feet long. It is filled with wood and covered with smooth stones, and then (49)
the wood is set aflame. The fire burns until the scorching hot stones rest on a bed of (67)
coals. The priest throws dried leaves onto the stones, and if they burst into flames, the (83)
pit is ready. The fires are so intense that spectators must stay thirty feet from the edge. (100)

The priest and his followers step onto the stones and slowly walk the full length (115)
of the pit, which can be heated to temperatures of more than nine hundred degrees (130)
Fahrenheit. The firewalkers use no protective oils or chemicals, but they are never (143)
burned or blistered, and there is no damage to their hair or clothing. (156)

Scientists have yet to come up with a satisfactory explanation for the remarkable (169)
feat. Some say that wood, ash, and feet are poor conductors of heat. In addition, the (185)
time of contact between feet and stones or coals is too quick for the coals to burn the (203)
walker. Another theory is that the circulation of blood through the feet helps to keep (218)
them cooler. Some scientists believe that state of mind is an important factor, so the (233)
firewalker's belief is essential. (237)

Words Correct Per Minute: _____

Assessing Fluency

Make-Believe

When you go to the movies, you can see dinosaurs roam through city streets. (14)
Humans fly to the rescue while aliens destroy skyscrapers with laser cannons. Waves (27)
hundreds of feet high drown continents. How do filmmakers do this? (38)

What you see on the screen is known as special effects. Artists and craftspeople (52)
who create the effects use science, technology, and a few tricks to make an audience (67)
accept make-believe as the real thing. (74)

The earliest form of special effects in film was discovered by accident. At the (88)
end of the nineteenth century, a filmmaker stopped his hand crank camera when (101)
the film jammed. When he developed the film he saw that the scene appeared to (116)
magically transform at the point the camera had stopped and started. When he used (130)
the technique to make a short film in which a girl in a chair turned into a skeleton, (148)
audiences were amazed. (151)

Another big step was model animation. Small, realistic clay models were filmed, (163)
then moved slightly and filmed again. The process was repeated again and again. This (177)
gave the appearance of the model moving on its own. Later developments included (190)
rolling film forward and in reverse and constructing miniatures for special scenes. An (203)
actor's makeup could be changed between takes to make the actor appear to age or (218)
become a monster right before the audience's eyes. (226)

Another technique, compositing, can make actors in a studio look like they are on (240)
Mars. Two images are shot separately, then layered one over the other. The person or (255)
object in front is shot against a plain blue screen. The blue is removed later so the (272)
background shows through. Today, computer-generated imaging, or CGI, can do things (284)
limited only by the filmmaker's imagination. (290)

Words Correct Per Minute: _____

Assessing Fluency

Caves

There are several definitions for the geological formation known as a cave. In (13)
general, it is a natural hollow space in the ground or rock, but some experts add that (30)
a cave should be large enough for a human to enter. Flowing underground water, wind, (45)
ice, ocean waves, or hardened tubes of lava may form caves. (56)

Moving water creates limestone caves. When rainwater falls through the air, it (68)
absorbs carbon dioxide and becomes slightly acidic. The rainwater seeps into the (80)
ground. If the rock layer is made of limestone, the acid in the groundwater slowly (95)
dissolves the layers of rock, creating underground openings. (103)

Once a cave or cavern is formed, groundwater continues to percolate down through (116)
the roof. Carrying dissolved minerals, the water may drip from the same spot, (129)
undisturbed for hundreds of years. As each drop eventually evaporates, it deposits (141)
minerals that dry and harden. Over time, incredible rock formations known as (153)
stalactites grow longer. The longest free-hanging stalactite known is almost forty feet (166)
in length! Some drops of water reach the cave floor, depositing minerals that become (180)
cones, ledges, and stacks called stalagmites. The tallest stalagmite known is nearly (192)
as tall as a ten-story building. The world's largest individual cave is in Malaysia. At (208)
its highest point it soars up twenty stories. Its widest point could hold seven football (223)
fields end to end. (227)

Words Correct Per Minute: _____

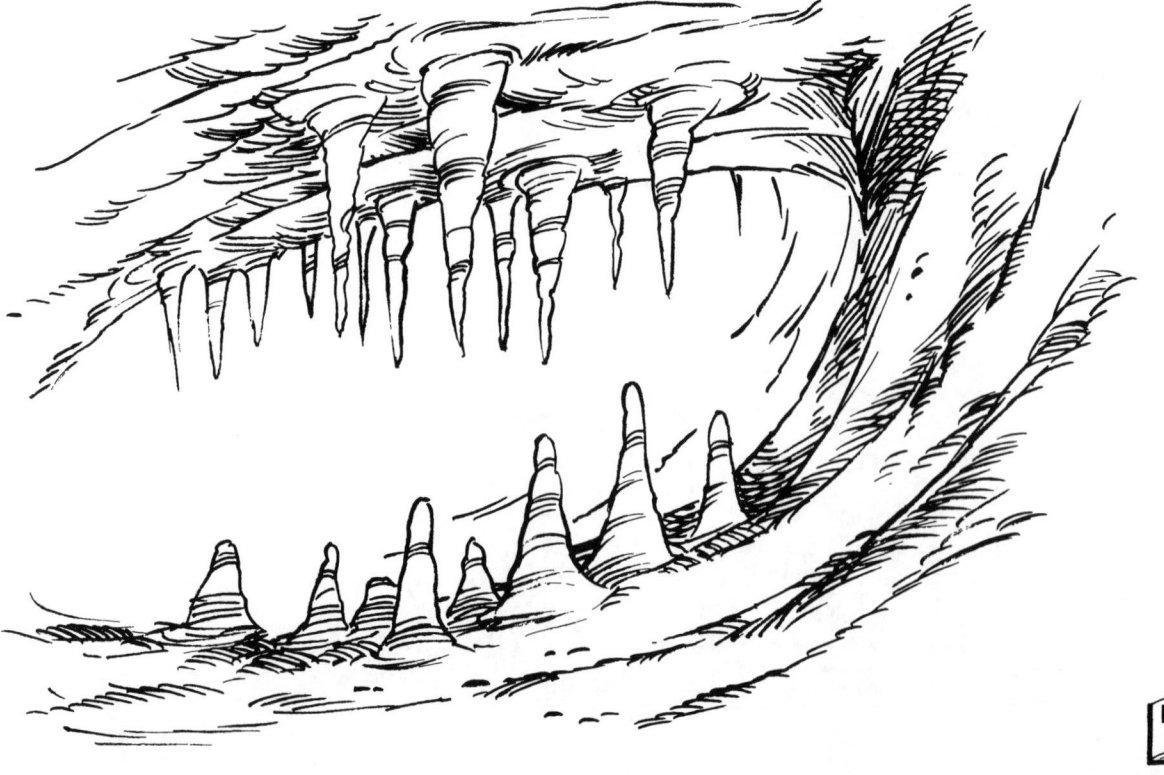

Assessing Fluency

A Great Saint

    High in the Swiss Alps, an imposing tenth-century monastery stands at a (13)
treacherous mountain pass. Led by a man who would be known to the world as St. (29)
Bernard, monks built the monastery and included a hospice where travelers could get (42)
help on the difficult journey across the mountain. Even in summer, the narrow trails (56)
were tricky to navigate. But in the harsh winter, they were nearly impossible. The snow (71)
and ice-covered terrain were extremely hazardous. Blizzards with gale-force winds and (84)
avalanches could turn it into a death trap where victims could be buried in an instant (100)
or freeze to death in blinding snowstorms. (107)

    The monks soon realized that their substantial dogs were well equipped to rescue (120)
unfortunate travelers. The sure-footed animals had warm coats, a remarkable sense (132)
of smell, and an uncanny sense of direction. The physically powerful dogs were sturdy (146)
and muscular as well as loyal and highly intelligent. They usually worked in pairs or (161)
even in groups. A pair might lie on the sides of a fallen traveler to insulate him from (179)
the freezing cold. They licked his face while another dog raced to the monastery to (194)
bring reinforcements. (196)

    Records show that the dogs rescued more than two thousand people. Among the (209)
best-known dogs was Barry. Sadly, thinking Barry was a bear, a boy stabbed him (224)
during a rescue. The monks found the injured dog, nursed him back to health, and sent (240)
him to the city to live out the rest of his years. About 1810, the St. Bernard dog was (259)
even referred to as a Barry hound, while today, one dog at the monastery is always (275)
named Barry in his honor. (280)

Words Correct Per Minute: _____

References

Allington, R. L. (1983). Fluency: The neglected goal. *The Reading Teacher, 36*, 556–561.

Campbell, K. U. (1996). *Great leaps reading.* Gainsville, FL: Diarmuid Inc.

Chall, J. S., & Dale, E. (1995). *Readability revisited: The new Dale-Chall readability formula.* Cambridge, MA: Brookline.

Fry, E. (2004). *1,000 instant words.* Westminister, CA: Teacher Created Resources.

Fuchs, L. S., Fuchs, D., Hops, M. K., & Jenkins, J. R. (2001). Oral reading fluency as an indicator of reading competence: A theoretical, empirical, and historical analysis. *Scientific Studies of Reading. 5*(3), 239–245.

Harris, A. J., & Sipay, E. R. (1985). *How to increase reading ability: A guide to developmental and remedial methods.* New York, NY: Longman.

Heckelman, R. G. (1969). A neurological-impress method of remedial reading instruction. *Academic Therapy, 4*(4), 277–282.

Howell, K. W., Zucker, S. H., & Morehead, M. K. (1994). *The multilevel academic skills inventory.* Paradise Valley, AZ: H & Z.

Ihnot, C. (2001). *Why read naturally?* Retrieved April 23, 2006, from the Read Naturally Web site: http://www.readnaturally.com.

Jenkins, J. R., Fuchs, L. S., Espin, C., Van den Broek, P., & Deno, S. L. (2000, February). *Effects of task format and performance dimension on word reading measures: Criterion validity, sensitivity to impairment, and context facilitation.* Paper presented at the Pacific Coast Research Conference, San Diego, CA.

Marston, D., & Magnusson, D. (1988). *Curriculum-based measurement: District level implementation.* Washington, DC: National Association of School Psychologists.

McEwan, E. K. (2002). *Teach them all to read: Catching the kids who fall through the cracks.* Thousand Oaks, CA: Corwin Press.

National Reading Panel. (2002). *Report of the National Reading Panel: Teaching children to read: An evidence-based assessment of the scientific research literature on reading and its implications for reading instruction: Reports of the subgroups.* Rockville, MD: National Institute of Child Health and Human Development.

Opitz, M. E., & Rasinski, T. V. (1998). *Good-bye round robin: 25 effective oral reading strategies.* Portsmouth, NH: Heinemann.

Rasinski, T. V. (2003). *The fluent reader.* New York, NY: Scholastic Professional Books.

Searfoss, L. (1975). Radio reading. *The Reading Teacher, 29*, 295–296.

Shefelbine, J. (1999). *Reading voluminously and voluntarily.* In Scholastic Reading Counts Research. New York, NY: Scholastic. Retrieved June 12, 1999, from http://apps.scholastic.com/readingcounts/research/voluminouslky/voluntarily.

Sitton, R. (2002). *Rebecca Sitton's spelling sourcebook for eighth grade teachers.* Scottsdale, AZ: Eggers Publishing, Inc.

Snow, C. E., Burns, M. S., & Griffin, P. (Eds.). (1998). *Preventing reading difficulties in young children.* Washington, DC: National Academy Press, Committee on the Prevention of Reading Difficulties in Young Children, Commission on Behavioral and Social Sciences and Education, National Research Council.

Tompkins, G. E. (1998). *Fifty literacy strategies: Step by step.* Upper Saddle River, NJ: Merrill.

Trelease, J. (2006). *The read-aloud handbook.* New York, NY: Penguin Books.

Printed in the United States
By Bookmasters

By Bookmasters